Let's Cook Something Good!

*Three Generations of Italian Classics
from Our Table to Yours*

CHEF BO FERRARA

Acknowledgments

First, I would like to thank my father, Carl Ferrara. He inspired me, and all of my best qualities came from him. I always knew if I followed in his footsteps and ended up half the man he was, I would always be happy. He was caring, hardworking, honest, generous, and had integrity.

The time spent growing up and working with my father in our family business had a big impact on my brother and me. He showed us both how to live a fulfilling life. Back then, no children went hungry in our neighborhood and a lot of our neighbors would run tabs and pay by the week or month. My father would keep the tabs in a tin box under the counter. He was truly a rich man, not in the money he took in but in all the tabs that mysteriously disappeared from the tin box when families fell on hard times. A good man will be happy with his life and the world around him, and he will want to look out for others and help them when he can.

Now a big thanks to my teachers, my mother, and my uncle Frank, the two amazing chefs in my life who truly inspired my passion to cook. Thank you to Daisy and Alberta for not only being a big part of creating our family memories and traditions, but for being such a special part of my life, and for nurturing me into an Italian foodie before it was fashionable.

Two others that I love and am grateful to are my uncles John Ferrara and Paul DeGearo. Thank you for all the hard work you both put in building my pizza and sub shop! I believe this was the catalyst that led me to where I am today.

A big thanks to my uncle, Frank Capone, cousins Joe DeGearo, Peggy DeGearo Senecal, Mark Senecal, and Moe Mahar for sharing your recipes. Thank you to the Ferrara and DeGearo families for your support!

Last, but certainly not least, a special thanks to Kimberly Cline for helping put this book together.

Creating Our Memories and Traditions

I remember the days of cooking with my mother, uncle Frank, Daisy, and Alberta — the old days. When we lived literally in the kitchen. I have wonderful memories of helping them cook our big family dinners. It was a sip here and a stir there. Although the food didn't always turn out perfectly, there was always a great story being shared. Those were the special memories that created our family traditions. Thank you for being such a special part of my life.

I hope that this cookbook helps you bring your family together in the kitchen, and back to your table. May this book also bring happiness to everyone inside the kitchen and out.

Chef Bo — Bon Appét

Uncle John & Baby Rory

Mom & Daisy and her husband

Cousin Joe & Alberta

Bo & Uncle Frank

Mom & Dad

Uncle Paul & Wife

Contents

Fried Calamari page 17

Crabcakes page 13

Sausage Mushrooms page 19

Apple & Pear Chutney page 12

Contents

Peppercorn Brandy Cream Sauce page 30

Citrus Sauce page 25

Creamy Carbonara Sauce page 26

Boscaiola Sauce page 24

Contents

Minestrone page 41

Polenta page 51

Parmesan Dauphinoise Potatoes page 52

Marinated Octopus Salad page 48

Contents

Simmered Red Wine Boston Pork page 58

Spicy Sausage and Red Wine Stew page 59

Veal and Peppers page 60

White Wine Simmered Chicken page 61

Contents

Steak Pizzaiola page 90

Sausage and Beef-Filled Cannelloni page 88

Veal Parmesan page 91

Contents

Almond Crescent Cookies page 102

Ricotta Lemon Drop Cookies page 109

Hot or Mild Italian Sausage page 96

Apple Pear Pie page 103

Great Beginnings

Apple & Pear Chutney

2 firm-ripe red Bartlett pears
2 Granny Smith apples
2 ounces butter
4 ounces onion; chopped
1/4 jalapeño (or to taste); chopped
3 ounces white wine
1 cup golden raisins; optional

1/2 cup white vinegar
1/4 cup water
1/3 cup sugar
1/4 teaspoon ground clove
1/2 teaspoon ground cinnamon
1/2 teaspoon ground allspice

Peel, core and halve the pears and apples. Cut 2 pear halves and 2 apple halves into 1/4 inch-thick slices and chop remaining pears and apples. In a 2-quart saucepan on medium heat, sauté onion and jalapeño in butter, deglaze with wine, and add the sliced and chopped pears and apples with remaining ingredients to the pan. Bring to a simmer, stirring gently. Simmer the chutney covered while stirring occasionally until fruit is just tender; this can take up to 30 minutes or more. Let chutney cool. The chutney can be made 1 day ahead, cover and chill. Serve chutney chilled or at room temperature.

Yield: 2 cups | Recipe by Chef Bo

Crabcakes

2½ cups mayonnaise
3 to 4 tablespoons whole grain mustard
2 tablespoons Old Bay seasoning
2 teaspoons Worcestershire sauce
2 or 3 dashes of Tabasco

2 tablespoons butter
1 small red and green pepper; diced
1/2 cup small onion; diced
3 pounds lump crab meat
5 cups ground Ritz crackers (more if needed)

Serve with my remoulade sauce. Recipe included in this book on page 33. The Ritz crackers are the key to these wonderful crabcakes.

In a large bowl, mix first 5 listed ingredients. Sauté the peppers and onions in butter. Cool slightly and add into the sauce mix. Gently stir in the crab meat. Add 3 cups of the ground crackers and gently mix, making sure to not break up the crab (add more cracker if needed). Shape into 20 patties: 2 inches wide and 1 inch thick (hockey pucks). Roll them in the remainder of ground crackers to cover all sides. Place on prepared sheet. Preheat flat top or large sauté pan to medium, lightly buttered. Place the crabcakes on the flat top or in the sauté pan for about 8 minutes on each side, or until golden brown on each side. Return to the sheet to keep them warm, or when ready to serve. Reheat in a 375-degree oven for 10 to 15 minutes.

Yield: 20 Crabcakes | Recipe by Chef Bo

Cousin Joe's Tadols

3/4 cup warm water
1/3 cup dry white wine
1/4 cup olive oil
4½ cups of flour
1 teaspoon instant yeast (bread machine yeast)

1¼ teaspoons salt
1/2 teaspoon sugar
1/8 cup fennel seeds
1 teaspoon black pepper; coarsely grated

Combine first three wet ingredients in a 2-cup measuring cup or small bowl, and heat in microwave until warm to the touch. Put all but 1/4 cup of flour in a large mixing bowl. Add remaining dry ingredients, and mix well with a whisk. Make a well in the dry ingredients. Add the wet ingredients, and mix well. I start mixing with a wooden spoon or stiff silicone spatula until most wet ingredients are incorporated so the dough does not stick to my hands. Add some additional flour, or warm water as necessary, to make a sticky dough. The dough should not stick to the counter when worked but is stickier than regular bread dough. Knead the dough for 8 to 10 minutes. Add a little more water if the dough is not smooth and elastic after a minute or two of kneading. Place in a greased bowl large enough to allow the dough to double in size. Cover and let rise in a warm area for about 1-1/2 hours or until double in size (or let it raise overnight at room temperature). Punch the dough down, and keep covered so it doesn't dry out. Break off chunks of dough that are large enough to form about six rings at a time, which would be about a 2"-diameter ball. Flatten and shape the ball so you can cut it into about a half dozen equal pieces. Using both hands, roll the cut dough pieces from the center out toward the ends to shape the dough into ropes that are about 7/16" diameter by 9" long. Then pinch the ends together to make a ring, and place the rings on a tray to dry. It is better to vary the length, not the diameter of each rope so the completed rings will bake evenly. Then starting from the oldest tray, boil them, a few at a time, in a pot of salted water. They will plump up a little during the boil. Just boil until they rise to the top, which should take 30 seconds or so. NOTE: If they float immediately, leave them in the water for at least 30 seconds before you remove them. After they float to the top, carefully remove them with a slotted spoon and place on a lint-free cloth like a folded tablecloth or kitchen towel. Let them set for a few minutes to absorb most of the water but not long enough to stick to the cloth. Remove them from the cloth, and place on a tray to air-dry. Depending on the humidity, air-drying could take several hours. When completely dry, put trays in oven and bake at 385-400 degrees for 15 to 20 minutes or until oven brown.

 Yield: 4 to 5 dozen | Recipe by Joe DeGearo   *Let's Cook Something Good*

Crispy Zucchini Fritters

1/2 cup plain yogurt
1 tablespoon lemon juice
2 garlic cloves; minced
2 teaspoons fresh dill or 1/2 teaspoon dried dill
Salt and pepper to taste
1 zucchini; shredded
1 egg; beaten
1/3 cup almond flour
4 ounces ricotta cheese
3 tablespoons Parmesan cheese; grated
1 tablespoon chives; freshly chopped
1 tablespoon parsley; freshly chopped

Keto-friendly oil for pan-frying

May also be served with my remoulade sauce. Recipe included in this book on page 33.

SAUCE

Make the dill sauce by mixing the yogurt, lemon juice, garlic, and dill together. Season with salt and pepper to taste.

FRITTERS

In a mixing bowl, combine the shredded zucchini, egg, almond flour, ricotta cheese, Parmesan cheese, chives, parsley as well as salt and pepper to taste. Stir to combine well. Heat a thin layer of (keto-friendly) cooking oil in a skillet over medium-high heat. Drop large tablespoons of the zucchini mixture into the heated oil in the skillet. Cook for 2 to 3 minutes on each side until golden brown and crispy on the outside. Remove the fritters from the oil, and place on a towel-lined plate to drain and cool. Serve with the dill sauce or your favorite (keto-friendly) dipping sauce such as ranch or sour cream.

Yield: 12 to 18 fritters | Recipe By Chef Bo

Fixed Greek Olives

4 cups unpitted Kalamata (Greek) olives; drained
1/2 cup olive oil
4 garlic cloves; sliced or chopped
1 tablespoon lemon juice

1 tablespoon oregano
3 teaspoons fennel seed
1/4 to 1/2 teaspoon crushed red pepper
   seeds to taste
Salt and pepper to taste

Place olives in a bowl, then combine the remaining ingredients, and pour over the olives and stir. Cover and refrigerate for 1 to 2 days before serving, stirring several times each day. Olives may be refrigerated for two weeks.

Yield: 1 quart | Recipe by Carl Ferarra Sr.

Fried Calamari & Mild Peppers

2 pounds fresh small to medium-sized squid;
    cleaned
3 to 4 cups oil for frying
3/4 cup cornstarch
3/4 cup flour
1/2 cup cornmeal

2 teaspoons salt
1 teaspoon pepper
1 cup buttermilk
16 to 20 sliced banana peppers in vinegar;
    drained
2 jalapeño; thinly sliced; optional

Serve with my remoulade sauce. Recipe included in this book on page 33.

Cut your calamari into ¼-inch rings, or leave the tentacles whole if you like. Place onto a rimmed baking sheet lined with paper towel, and cover with additional paper towel. Place in fridge for 1 hour to dry.

In a large bowl, mix the ingredients for the breading (cornstarch, flour, cornmeal, salt, and pepper), and set aside. Pour the buttermilk into a medium bowl. Add the dried calamari, peppers, and jalapeño (if using) to the buttermilk. Make sure all the pieces are well coated. Working in batches, use a large slotted spoon or strainer to transfer 1/4 of the squid to the flour mixture. Make sure to drain off as much buttermilk as possible first. Use your hands to gently toss the calamari in the flour, ensuring every piece is covered and none are sticking together. Preheat your oil to 365 degrees in a 3-quart frying pan. Gently shake off the excess flour, and carefully place into the hot oil. Fry until golden brown, usually around 50 seconds. Your best bet is to fry one or two pieces first, until you get the timing right. These cook very quickly, and if overcooked become extremely rubbery. Transfer the cooked calamari to a paper towel set over a rimmed baking sheet. Let the oil come back up to temperature, then repeat with remaining batch(es). When all the calamari have been fried, place on a plate to serve immediately.

Yield: 4 to 6 servings | Recipe by Chef Bo

Pizza Dough

1½ cups warm water
1 envelope dry yeast
2 tablespoons olive oil
1 teaspoon sugar
2 teaspoons salt
4 cups flour

Mix water and yeast for about 5 minutes. Add oil, sugar, salt, and mix well. Add flour, then beat until the dough forms into a ball. If the dough is too sticky, just add a little more flour. Place the dough onto a lightly floured surface, flatten, and gently knead back into a smooth firm ball. Grease a large bowl with olive oil, then add the dough to the bowl, and cover with a towel or plastic wrap. Place in a warm spot to let double in size for about one hour, then place the dough on a lightly floured surface. Divide into 2 equal pieces, then cover each with a towel and let them rest for about 10 minutes. Now Let's Roll!

Yield: (2) 14-inch pies | Recipe by Chef Bo

Sausage Stuffed Mushrooms

24 large mushrooms; stems removed and diced
3/4 cup white wine; divided
1 pound bulk mild or sweet Italian sausage
1 small onion; diced
1 teaspoon garlic; minced

Diced stems
4 ounces grated Parmesan cheese; divided
1 to 2 cups ground Ritz crackers
1 teaspoon fresh parsley; chopped
1/2 cup melted butter; optional

Preheat oven to 350 degrees. Place the mushroom caps in a 9x15 baking dish, and drizzle the caps with 1/2 cup of the wine. Bake about 10 minutes, then remove the pan from the oven and set aside to cool. In a skillet over medium-high heat, add sausage (out of casing), onions, garlic, and diced mushroom stems. Cook in hot skillet until sausage is browned for about 8 to 10 minutes. Drain 1/2 the grease, and transfer the mixture into a 3-quart bowl. Add 3 ounces of the Parmesan cheese, 1/2 the Ritz crackers, parsley, and mix. If too loose, add more Ritz, and if too dry, add some melted butter. Roll the stuffing into 24 balls, and press each ball into a mushroom cap. Place back in the baking pan. Drizzle the mushroom caps with the remaining wine, and return the mushrooms back to the oven and bake for 10 minutes. Sprinkle with the remaining 1 ounce of Parmesan cheese, and return the mushrooms back to the oven and bake for 5 more minutes.

Yield: 24 stuffed mushrooms | Recipe by Chef Bo

Let's Get Saucy

Alfredo Sauce (No Cream)

Let's get creative~ what's in your sauté pan? As your pasta is cooking, you can create a new Alfredo dish every time just by sautéing one or more of these and adding it to your warm bowl: chicken, shrimp, lobster, pork sausage, chicken sausage, garlic, sun-dried tomatoes, roasted red peppers, asparagus, broccoli, mushrooms, or my favorite diced red onions and bacon for a quick Carbonara.

1 pound soft butter, room temperature
1 pound imported grated Parmesan cheese, room temperature
1 pound fettuccine
1 or 2 tablespoons of cracked black pepper for topping
1/2 cup of grated Parmesan cheese for topping
one sauté pan
one large warm bowl

Take the equal parts of the soft butter and freshly grated Parmesan cheese all at room temperature and place in a mixing bowl and whip till creamy about 5 to 8 minutes. Cook the fettuccine. As soon as the pasta is done, add the hot fettuccine right out of the water and add 8 ounces of the room-temperature Alfredo sauce, and add any other options you may have chosen to sauté to the hot bowl. Now toss the pasta and sauce together, and plate. Top with a few grinds of cracked black pepper and more cheese if you like, and serve.

This is the true Alfredo sauce. I like to make the sauce this way because the sauce can be saved by refrigeration or by freezing. You can double, triple, or make even larger if you like.

Helpful hints: This version of Alfredo sauce can never be heated; always use this version of Alfredo sauce as a fold-in at room temperature. You can warm the bowl by using some of the hot pasta water. Also, this sauce is harder to make in cold weather. I sometimes if needed will keep a hair dryer on a medium to low heat blowing on my mixing bowl.

Yield: 16 servings | Recipe by Chef Bo

Amazing Pizza Sauce

1/3 cup olive oil	1 tablespoon dried oregano
5 garlic cloves; minced	1/2 teaspoon salt
1/2 ounce ground fennel seed	1/4 teaspoon black pepper
1 (28 ounce) can crushed tomatoes	1/2 teaspoon crushed red pepper; optional
4½ ounces tomato paste	3/4 can of water from rinsing the can
1/2 teaspoon dried basil	1 oz Parmesan cheese or more to taste

Store the pizza sauce in a jar or airtight container in the refrigerator for up to 1 week, or freeze for up to 3 months.

In a saucepan, heat the olive oil over medium heat. Add the garlic, and sauté for one minute, add the fennel, and sauté one minute, add crushed tomatoes, tomato paste, basil, oregano, salt, and black pepper, red pepper (optional) if using and water. Stir until combined, and simmer over low heat for 10 minutes. You can simmer for up to 20 minutes, if you want.

Cool 20 minutes, add cheese. Store the pizza sauce in a jar or airtight container in the refrigerator for up to one week, or cool completely and freeze for up to three months.

Yield: 1½ quarts | Recipe by Chef Bo and Uncle Frank

Boscaiola (Lumberjack) Sauce

6 ounces of pancetta or bacon
2¼ pounds of mixed wild mushrooms such as cremini, shiitake, maitake, or oyster ends trimmed; thinly sliced
2 ounces porcini mushrooms; diced
1/4 cup of olive oil
1 medium onion; diced
6 garlic cloves; chopped

2 teaspoons fresh thyme leaves
2/3 cup white wine
2 quarts heavy cream plus 1 cup water to rinse out containers
1½ cups marinara (recipe on page 28)
1 tablespoon salt and black pepper to taste
Pappardelle noodle

In a large saucepan, cook the bacon over a medium heat until brown for about 5 to 8 minutes. Using a slotted spoon, transfer bacon to a plate. Add fresh mushrooms and porcini to the saucepan with the bacon fat. Return to medium-high heat, stirring often until mushrooms are browned, for about 10 minutes. Add the olive oil, onions, garlic, and thyme, then cook until onions are soft and lightly browned, for about 6 to 8 minutes. Add the wine to deglaze, and reduce by half. Add the bacon back to the pan. Add the cream, marinara, salt and pepper, then simmer on low to reduce the cream until the desired thickness. Meanwhile, bring a pot of salted water to a boil, and cook your pappardelle noodles al dente, and top with your sauce.

Yield: 2 quarts | Recipe by Chef Bo

Citrus Sauce

1 cup orange juice
1 cup pineapple juice
1 cup grapefruit juice
4 ounces lime juice

6 ounces heavy cream
1½ pounds softened butter; cut in small pieces
Salt and pepper to taste

In a 3-quart heavy or thick saucepan on medium heat, add all the citrus juices and reduce to almost a paste. You must stand over this sauce while stirring and watch so it will not burn. Add cream, and reduce by half. Reduce the heat to very low. Whip in the soft butter one piece at a time. Do not add another piece till the previous piece is dissolved. Finish with salt and pepper if you like.

Yield: 2 cups | Recipe by Chef Bo

This sauce is amazing. It is so versatile and has such a wide range of uses from putting it on your grilled mahi, to topping your ice cream. You will love it. But it is a labor of love to make.

Creamy Carbonara Sauce

4 eggs
1/2 cup cream or heavy whipping cream
1/4 cup pecorino Romano cheese
1/4 cup Parmesan
1/4 teaspoon salt

Sprinkling of red pepper flakes
1/2 pound pancetta or bacon
1/4 cup red onion; chopped
1 pound spaghetti
2 cups of saved pasta cooking water

Beat the eggs, cream, Romano, Parmesan, salt, and red pepper flakes together in a bowl. This can be done with a fork. In a large skillet, fry the bacon until crisp, then crumble and set aside. In a large saucepan on medium heat, use 1 or 2 tablespoons of the bacon grease and sauté the onions until they are translucent, not browned. Set onions aside. Cook the pasta in salted water, then drain the pasta and, while still warm, add to the saucepan that the onions are in. Pour the cream mixture over the pasta and stir. Cook the mixture on a low heat for two minutes or until sauce thickens. Don't do this on high heat. I save a bit of the pasta water just in case the sauce gets thicker than I like. Simply add a bit of the water if you need it.

Yield: 4 to 6 servings | Recipe by Chef Bo

Gorgonzola and Walnuts Cream Sauce

4 tablespoons unsalted butter
6 ounces mild Gorgonzola cheese
1 cup heavy cream
3/4 cup Parmesan; freshly grated & chopped
Pinch of nutmeg

1/2 teaspoon freshly ground pepper
1 pound penne pasta
1/2 cup walnuts; lightly toasted & coarsely chopped

I like this sauce with penne pasta.

Bring a large pot of salted water to a boil over high heat. In a large frying pan over medium-low heat, melt the butter. Stir in the Gorgonzola, mashing the cheese as it heats. Add the cream, and bring to a gentle simmer, stirring occasionally. Reduce the heat to low, and cook, stirring, until the sauce is thickened for about 3 to 4 minutes. Do not allow the sauce to boil. Remove from the heat, and stir in the Parmesan, nutmeg, and pepper. Meanwhile, cook the pasta while stirring occasionally until al dente for about 10 minutes. Drain, reserving about 1/2 cup of the cooking water. Add the pasta to the sauce along with the walnuts, and stir to combine. Add as much of the reserved cooking water as needed to loosen the sauce. Reheat briefly over low heat, and serve.

Yield: 4 to 6 servings | Recipe by Chef Bo

Marinara Sauce

1/4 cup extra-virgin olive oil
3 to 4 cloves of garlic; chopped
1 small onion; chopped fine
2 (28 ounces) cans crushed tomatoes; use a
  quality brand
2 (6 ounces) cans tomato paste
1½ to 2 cups water; use to rinse the tomato can

4 or 5 fresh basil leaves
1/2 cup chopped fresh parsley
Salt and pepper to taste
1/2 teaspoon sugar; optional
  (Sometimes I will add a little diced carrots
  to the garlic and onions to add just the right
  sweetness to the sauce.)

In a large saucepan, add the oil, garlic, and onions. Cook on medium heat until garlic and onions are soft or lightly browned. Add crushed tomatoes, tomato paste, and water. Cook on medium to medium-high uncovered for 20 minutes. Add the basil, parsley, salt and pepper to taste, and 1/2 teaspoon sugar (optional). Simmer 10 to 12 more minutes.

Yield: 3 quarts | Recipe by Chef Bo

Mushroom Marsala Sauce

2 ounces butter
3 shallots; finely chopped or one small red onion
2 garlic cloves; finely chopped
A pinch of crushed red pepper or to taste
4 ounces portobello mushrooms; diced
1½ pounds mushrooms; sliced

8 ounces Marsala wine
2 quarts warm brown sauce (demi-glace preferred; try Minor's Concentrate Demi-Glace on Amazon)
Salt and pepper to taste
2 ounces soft butter to finish

Melt first listed butter in a 3 to 4-qt saucepan on a medium heat. Add shallots or onion, garlic, red pepper, and cook 3 to 4 minutes. Add the mushrooms, and cook for an additional 5 to 8 minutes. Turn the heat to high, add the wine to deglaze pan and reduce by half, then turn the heat back down. Add the warm demi-glace, salt and pepper, and heat back to a simmer. Turn off the heat and whip in the second listed butter to finish.

Yield: 2 quarts | Recipe by Chef Bo

A Quick Brown Sauce for this Recipe
6 tablespoons vegetable oil
8 ounces of red onion chopped or 8 ounces of mirepoix (equal part diced onion. carrot, celery)
2 tablespoons garlic chopped
6 tablespoons of flour
3 tablespoons tomato pasta
8 cups beef stock
Salt and pepper to taste

Add oil to a heavy saucepan on medium heat, add the onions or mirepoix and garlic, and sauté for 2 to 3 minutes, add flour and cook for about 1 minute, add tomato pasta and beef stock, and cook down slowly until the sauce thickens.

You can thicken the sauce if needed by adding small amounts of roux slowly while the sauce is still simmering. Roux is equal parts flour and fat, typically melted butter mixed and cooked for 3 to 5 minutes for a light Roux, 8 to 15 minutes for a brown or dark roux. Typically used in Cajun cooking like gumbo.

Peppercorn Brandy Cream Sauce

1 ounce butter
1/2 tablespoon shallots; chopped
5 ounces green canned peppercorn; drained
3 ounces cognac or brandy

1 cup heavy cream
3 cups brown sauce (demi-glace preferred); try Minor's Concentrate Demi-Glace on Amazon
Salt and pepper to taste

In a 3-quart saucepan on medium heat, sauté the butter, shallots, and peppercorns for 3 minutes. Turn the heat up and add the cognac to deglaze for one minute or less. Add the cream and reduce by half. Add the demi-glace and reduce to a good consistency. Add salt and pepper.

Yield: 1 quart | Recipe by Chef Bo

A Quick Brown Sauce for this Recipe
6 tablespoons vegetable oil
8 ounces of red onion chopped or 8 ounces of mirepoix; equal part diced onion, carrot, celery
2 tablespoons garlic chopped
6 tablespoons of flour
3 tablespoons tomato pasta
8 cups beef stock
Salt and pepper to taste

Add oil to a heavy saucepan on medium heat, add the onions or mirepoix and garlic, and sauté for 2 to 3 minutes, add flour and cook for about 1 minute, add tomato pasta and beef stock, and cook down slowly until the sauce thickens.

Pork Butt, Sausage, and Meatball Sauce

3/4 cup of extra-virgin olive oil
2 to 4 pounds bone-in pork butt
6 to 8 garlic cloves; chopped
2 medium onions; chopped fine
4 to 6 Ferrara's sausage links
3 (28 ounces) cans of crushed tomatoes;
    use a quality brand

3 (6 ounces) cans tomato paste
3 cups water (use to rinse the tomato cans)
Salt and pepper to taste
3/4 teaspoon sugar; optional
6 to 8 Sicilian meatballs (recipe on page 54)
6 to 7 fresh basil leaves
3/4 cup fresh parsley; chopped

This version of sauce is another labor of love to make.

in a very large saucepan on medium-high, add the oil, and pork butt, brown on all sides, and remove. Add garlic, onions, and the sausage. Cook for 8 minutes, stirring frequently to ensure you evenly brown the sausage. Add the pork butt back to the pan, add crushed tomatoes, tomato paste, and water, and simmer while stirring frequently on medium heat uncovered for 50 to 70 minutes (depending on the size of your pork butt). Lower heat slightly, and add meatballs, basil, parsley, salt and pepper to taste, and sugar; (optional), stirring carefully to not break up the meatballs. Simmer 20 to 25 minutes longer, adding water if the sauce is getting too thick. At this time, the meatballs should have finished cooking and the pork butt should be fork-tender. Skim off grease as needed.

Yield: 8 to 12 servings | Recipe by Chef Bo

Red Clam Sauce

3 (6.5 ounce) cans whole clams
16 fresh little neck clams; rinsed
1/4 cup extra-virgin olive oil
6 cloves garlic; chopped
One medium onion; chopped
Small pinch red pepper flakes to taste
1 cup clam juice

1 (28 ounce) can crushed tomatoes
2 tablespoons tomato paste
1 pound dry linguini
1½ teaspoons oregano
2 tablespoons parsley; finely chopped
Kosher salt

Drain the clams, save their juice, and set aside. Heat the olive oil in a 3-quart saucepan over medium-low heat. Add the garlic, onion, and cook until softened for about 3 minutes, do not brown. Add red pepper flake,s and cook for 30 seconds. Add one cup of the saved clam juice, tomatoes, and tomato paste. Increase the heat just to bring the sauce to a slow simmer. Cover and lower the heat to maintain a gentle simmer, cook for 20 minutes, and set aside. Bring a large pot of salted water to a boi,l and cook the pasta until al dente. During the last 8 minutes of cooking the pasta, stir in the oregano and parsley into the clam sauce. Bring back to a slow simmer for 4 to 5 minutes. Add the canned clams, fresh clams, and remaining clam juice to the sauce. Cover and bring back to a simmer for 3 minutes, keep covered and remove from heat not to make the clam tough and adjust the salt. Drain the pasta, toss with the sauce, top each plate with a few clam shells, and serve.

Yield: 4 to 6 servings | Recipe by Chef Bo

Remoulade Sauce

1 cup mayonnaise
1/4 cup chili sauce
2 tablespoons Creole mustard
2 tablespoons extra-virgin olive oil
1 tablespoon Louisiana-style hot sauce or
   to taste
2 tablespoons fresh lemon juice
1 teaspoon Worcestershire sauce
4 medium scallions; chopped

2 tablespoons fresh parsley; chopped
2 tablespoons green olives; chopped
2 tablespoons celery; minced
1 teaspoon capers; chopped; optional
1 clove garlic; minced
1/2 teaspoon chili powder
1 teaspoon salt or to taste
1/2 teaspoon ground black pepper

Top or dip your fried calamari, crab, shrimp, or lobster, or top your shrimp po' boy sandwiches with this wonderful sauce that has its origins in France and was then popularized in New Orleans.

Mix together in a bowl the mayonnaise, chili sauce, mustard, olive oil, hot sauce, lemon juice, and Worcestershire sauce. Stir in scallions, parsley, olives, celery, capers, garlic, chili powder, salt and pepper, and mix. Cover and refrigerate for 2 hours or more before using.

Yield: 1-3/4 cups | Recipe by Chef Bo

Roasted Red Pepper Purée

1/4 cup of oil
15 red peppers
2 ounces garlic
2 ounces white wine
4 ounces olive oil
Salt and pepper to taste

Rub peppers with some oil, and roast pepper over open flame or under a broiler until black on all sides, turning frequently. Place in a bowl while hot, and cover with plastic wrap for 15 to 20 minutes. Peel off black skin, and remove the seeds and let cool. In a blender, purée the peppers, add the garlic and wine, and purée a little more. Add the olive oil, salt and pepper, and purée a little more. Put in a squeeze bottle.

Yield: about 3 cups | Recipe by Chef Bo

Roasted Red Pepper Aioli

1/4 cup of olive oil
5 medium red peppers
4 garlic cloves; chopped fine
2/3 cup good mayonnaise
4 tablespoons olive oil
Salt and pepper to taste

Rub peppers with some oil, and roast pepper over open flame or under a broiler until black on all sides, place in a bowl while hot, and cover with saran wrap for 15 to 20 minutes. Peel off black skin and remove the seeds and let cool. Add the garlic in food processor, add the roasted peppers, and blend until smooth. Blend in the mayonnaise, reduce the speed, and with the processor running, blend in the oil. Add the salt and pepper, and put in a squeeze bottle.

Yield: about 2 cups | Recipe by Chef Bo

Serve as a dip or a spread for crabcakes, fried seafood, sweet potato fries, sandwiches, grilled chicken or fish. Can be stored for 2 days.

Spicy Bolognese Sauce

1/4 cup of extra-virgin olive oil
3 ounces Pancetta; optional
3 to 4 garlic cloves; chopped
1 small onion; chopped fine
1 medium carrot; chopped
1 medium celery stalk; chopped
1½ pounds ground beef
1½ pounds my mild loose sausage
1 cup red wine

2 (28 ounces) cans of crushed tomatoes; use a quality brand
2 (6 ounce) cans tomato paste
1½-2 cups water; use to rinse the tomato cans
4 or 5 fresh basil leaves
1/2 cup fresh parsley; chopped
Salt and pepper to taste

In a large saucepan on medium heat, add olive oil and pancetta if using and cook 2 to 3 minutes. Add garlic, onions, carrots, and celery to the saucepan. Cook on medium heat until lightly browned. Add ground beef and sausage, then cook until the meat is just done, breaking and chopping the meat as it is cooking. Drain off half the grease, add the wine to the meat, and reduce by half. Add crushed tomatoes, tomato paste, and water. Cook on medium to medium high uncovered for 30 minutes. Add the basil, parsley, and salt and pepper to taste. Simmer 10 to 12 more minutes.

Yield: 8 servings | Recipe by Chef Bo

Sun-dried Tomato Prosciutto Cream Sauce

3 tablespoons butter
1/4 pound prosciutto; julienned
6 ounces sun-dried tomato; julienned or diced
1 tablespoon garlic; chopped
1/3 cup white wine
1½ quarts of half-and-half or whipping cream
3 or 4 large fresh basil leaves; chopped

1/2 cup Romano or Parmesan cheese; grated
Salt and pepper to taste
1/4 cup (or to taste) Chef Bo's sun-dried tomato Pastika; optional
1 pound penne pasta
1/4 cup Romano or Parmesan cheese; grated
1 pound roasted red pepper or sun-dried tomato chicken sausage; optional

Bucatini pasta pairs great with this amazing sauce.

In a 3-quart saucepan on medium heat, add the butter, prosciutto, and sauté until slightly crisp. Add sun-dried tomato and garlic, and sauté two or three minutes. Deglaze with white wine, add cream, and slowly reduce by 1/2 or until thickened. Finish with fresh basil, first-listed cheese, salt and pepper, and Pastika (optional). Simmer on low for 6 to 8 minutes. As the sauce is simmering, cook your pasta in salted water al dente. Drain the pasta well, and toss with sauce. Top each plate with a sprinkle of the second-listed grated cheese.

Optional: Grill or sauté 1 pound Ferrara's roasted red pepper or sun-dried tomato chicken sausage. (Always cook on low to medium heat.) Cut your sausage into 1-inch slices, and top your pasta or toss it into the pasta.

Yield: 4 to 6 servings | Recipe by Chef Bo

Sun-dried Tomato Pesto Sauce

5 ounces sun-dried tomatoes
3 cloves of garlic
3 ounces basil
1 ounce walnuts
1½ ounces pine nuts
1 ounce Romano cheese or more to taste

Pinch of salt
Pinch of black pepper
1½ cups olive oil
16 ounces pasta
Pinch of red pepper flakes; optional
More Romano cheese

Put the first 8 ingredients in a small Robot Coupe (food processor) and purée. On a lower speed, slowly incorporate the olive oil until the right consistency is reached. In a small saucepan, heat the pesto on low, do not bring to a boil. Cook the pasta al dente in a large pot of boiling salted water, stirring occasionally, and drain. Toss the pasta and the pesto together, and serve. Season the pasta to taste with the Romano cheese. (Red pepper flakes optional)

Yield: 1 pint | Recipe by Chef Bo

Let's Cook Something Good

Soup for the Soul

Escarole and/or Broccoli Rabe & Beans

3 tablespoons extra-virgin olive oil
4 to 6 cloves garlic; crushed
2 to 3 ounces of pancetta or bacon; chopped
1¼ pounds loose sweet Italian sausage
1 medium onion; chopped
4 cups escarole or broccoli rabe: washed and
  coarsely chopped

2 (14 ounces) cans cannellini beans; drained
1 quart prepared chicken stock or broth
Salt and red or black pepper to taste
Shaved Parmigiano-Reggiano for topping

In a large heavy saucepan over moderate heat, sauté garlic and pancetta in extra-virgin olive oil for 3 minutes, then add the sausage and onions, and sauté for 5 to 8 minutes, breaking up the sausage as it cooks. Add the greens, and wilt them down to fit them all in the pot. Add beans, broth, salt, and pepper. Cook over moderate to medium-high heat for 20 minutes, or until greens are no longer bitter. Serve with Romano cheese, crusty bread for sopping, and a good red wine.

Yield: 3 quarts | Recipe by Chef Bo

Minestrone

2 tablespoons extra-virgin olive oil
4 ounces pancetta or bacon cut into
   1/8-inch pieces
1 cup chopped yellow onion
1½ cups sliced or diced carrots
1 cup sliced or diced celery
1 cup sliced or diced zucchini
1 cup chopped cabbage
1 cup chopped greens; kale or endive
4 garlic cloves, minced
1 teaspoon dried basil
1 teaspoon chopped fresh rosemary
4 or 5 fresh thyme stems
1 teaspoon salt
1/2 teaspoon fresh ground pepper

6 cups chicken broth
2 cups water
8 ounces dry red wine
1 bay leaf
1½ cups of fresh cut green beans
2 (14 ounces) cans cannellini beans; drained
1 (14 ounces) can kidney or
   garbanzo beans; drained
1 (14 ounces) can diced tomatoes; do not drain
1 (12 ounces) can tomato paste
1-1/3 cups dry ditalini pasta; cooked
Parmesan cheese for serving
Salt to taste
1 pound ditalini pasta
3 cups paste water / saved from cooking pasta

Top with fresh Parmesan cheese, if desired when serving. Want to make this a vegetarian soup? Omit the bacon and chicken broth, and use vegetable stock.

Heat the olive oil over medium heat in a 4-quart saucepan. Cook the pancetta for 3 to 4 minutes. Add the onion, carrots, celery, zucchini, cabbage, greens, garlic, basil, rosemary, thyme, salt, and pepper. Stir and cook for 6 to 7 minutes as the vegetables soften up and let out some juices. Add broth, water, red wine, bay leaf, fresh green beans, all the canned beans, diced tomatoes, and tomato paste. Bring to a boil, cover, and simmer for 35 minutes. As the soup is simmering, cook your pasta. NOTE: Never add the pasta to the soup; always add the pasta to the dish at time of serving. Remove the bay leaf and thyme stems before serving.

Yield: 8 to 10 servings | Recipe by Chef Bo

Pasta Fagioli

3 teaspoons olive oil
3/4 pound bacon; diced
3 teaspoons garlic; chopped
1/2 pound mild or sweet sausage out of the casing
1/4 pound fatty capocollo; diced
4 onions baseball size; sliced
3 cups celery hearts just whites and yellows; sliced
3/4 cup water or red wine
1 cup celery regular; sliced
1/4 cup fatty capocollo; cubed
2 (28 ounces) cans crushed tomatoes

1 can of water (from rinsing cans)
1 stick of good pepperoni; sliced
   1/2 inch thick
4 small ham hocks; optional
3 (16 ounces) cans of cannellini beans
3/4 cup parsley
2 teaspoons black pepper
Salt to taste
1 pound ditalini pasta
3 cups pasta water saved from cooking pasta

In a 6-quart saucepan, sauté bacon in olive oil on medium-high until light brown. Add garlic, sausage, and first-listed capocollo, and cook 6 or 8 more minutes, breaking up the sausage as it cooks. Add the onions and celery hearts. Sauté on medium-high, stirring frequently. This might take 20 minutes to cook the vegetables down. They will make water first but, as you continue to sauté, the sizzling sound will come back. The vegetables will be about 2 inches thick by this time and you should be getting some brown build-up on the bottom of the pan — this is good. Kick the heat up and keep stirring and scraping the bottom of the pan. Just before the pan starts to burn, deglaze with the wine or water.

Boil the liquid for 2 to 3 minutes as you keep scraping the brown off the bottom of the pan. Add the second-listed capocollo, tomatoes, water, sliced pepperoni, and ham hocks if using. Simmer for 20 minutes, and add beans, parsley, black pepper, and salt, and simmer 15 minutes more. At this point, your soup is almost done. Now start cooking your pasta. Cook the ditalini for 9 to 10 minutes for al dente, drain and save 3 cups of the cooking water. Now you can break up the ham hock if used or place one on each plate and pour your soup over them. Your soup should be on the thick side. If needed, you can thin the soup by using the hot water you saved from cooking the pasta. Now add about 1/2 cup or more of pasta to your plate. Ladle the soup over your pasta. Serve with Romano cheese, crusty bread for sopping, and a good red wine.

Yield: 3 quarts | Recipe by Chef Bo

Let's Cook Something Good

Sherry Cream of Mushroom Soup

3 pounds of white or cremini mushroom caps;
   sliced
4 tablespoons butter
1 large yellow onion, chopped
5 chopped shallots
1¼ cup dry sherry; optional
Marsala
5 tablespoons flour

6 cups whole milk
2 (14 ounces) cans of chicken broth
2 teaspoons Worcestershire sauce
1 teaspoon fresh thyme
Salt and pepper to taste
3 to 5 drops of Tabasco sauce; optional

Wipe mushroom caps with a damp cloth. Trim stems, and slice the mushroom caps. In a 4-quart pot on medium heat, melt butter, add onion and shallots, and sauté for about 2 minutes. Add mushrooms, and sauté for about 5 more minutes. Add the sherry and cook over medium-heat, stirring occasionally for about 8 to 10 minutes or until liquid is reduced by half. Sift the flour into the mix, and stir in, add in the milk, broth, Worcestershire sauce, thyme, salt, and pepper. Bring to a boil, then reduce heat and simmer on low for about 20 minutes or until the soup reaches the desired thickness, stirring occasionally. Stir in the optional Tabasco sauce.

Yield: 8 servings | Recipe by Chef Bo

Zucchini and Green Bean Stew

20 fresh green beans cut in 1 inch
3 tablespoons olive oil
4 slices of bacon; diced
3 cloves garlic; chopped
1 medium onion
2 (28 ounces) cans crushed tomatoes

1 can of water from rinsing can
1 (6 ounces) can tomato paste, plus one can of water from can
1 stick pepperoni diced; optional
2 medium zucchini; sliced 1/2 moons or large cubes
2 teaspoons basil; chopped
3 teaspoons parsley
1 teaspoon salt
Pinch of red pepper seeds; optional

Cut the fresh green beans into 1-inch pieces, blanch them lightly, and set them aside. Sauté bacon in olive oil in a 5-quart saucepan for 5 minutes, add the garlic and onion, and cook for 5 to 8 minutes. Add tomatoes, paste, water, and pepperoni, and simmer for 15 minutes. Add zucchini, green beans, basil, parsley, salt, and red pepper, and simmer for 18 to 20 minutes or until green beans are tender.

Yield: 3 1/2 quarts | Recipe by Madeline Phillips

Let's Cook Something Good

Salads & Sides

Chef Bo's Red Wine Mushrooms

6 tablespoons olive oil
4 garlic cloves; minced
1½ pounds fresh whole cremini mushrooms
1½ pounds portobello mushrooms; sliced; optional
4 tablespoons balsamic vinegar

1/2 cup red wine
1/4 teaspoon parsley
1/4 teaspoon basil
Pinch red pepper seeds; optional
Salt and pepper to taste

In a large skillet, sauté the garlic in olive oil for 1 to 2 minutes. Do not brown the garlic. Add mushrooms, and cook 3 more minutes, stirring occasionally. Add in balsamic vinegar, wine, parsley, and basil. Reduce the wine mixture by half or more. Add the optional red pepper seeds, salt, and pepper, and simmer 1 or 2 minutes and serve.

Yield: 4 to 6 servings | Recipe by Chef Bo

Farfalle Pasta Salad

1 pound farfalle pasta
1 cup olive oil
2 tablespoons fresh garlic; minced
2 cups grape or cherry tomatoes; halved
1 cup red bell pepper; diced
1 cup green bell pepper; diced

3/4 cup red onion; diced
1/4 cup fresh basil; chopped
1/2 teaspoon ground black pepper
3 tablespoons olive oil
1/2 cup feta cheese crumbles or shredded Parmesan

In a large stockpot, bring salted water to a boil over high heat. Add pasta, and cook for 9 minutes. Rinse in cold water, and cool down. Transfer to a large bowl, then stir in the olive oil, garlic, tomatoes, bell pepper, onions, basil, and black pepper. Toss to combine, and let cool in the refrigerator overnight. Just before serving, add the olive oil and cheese, and toss to combine.

Yield: 12 sides | Recipe by Chef Bo

Marinated Octopus Salad

6 cups water
1/2 cup white wine vinegar
1/2 cup fresh lemon juice
2 tablespoons kosher salt plus more to taste
4 dried bay leaves
4 fresh or frozen and thawed
  baby octopuses; cleaned

1/2 cup extra-virgin olive oil, plus more to taste
1 teaspoon dried oregano; preferably Greek
1 garlic clove; minced
Mixed salad greens for serving
Freshly ground black pepper to taste

In a 4-qt. saucepan, bring the water, vinegar, 3 tablespoons of the lemon juice, 2 tablespoons salt, and bay leaves to a boil. Cut each baby octopus into 5 pieces and add to the pan. Reduce heat to medium-low, and simmer while stirring occasionally until tender for about 30 to 45 minutes. Let the octopus cool in some of the cooking water. Transfer octopus to a large bowl, and toss with remaining lemon juice, olive oil, oregano, and garlic. Cover with plastic wrap, and refrigerate for at least 4 to 8 hours, preferably overnight. To serve, put greens on a platter, top with octopus, and season with salt and pepper.

Yield: 4 servings | Recipe by Chef Bo

Onion Olives Fish Pie

One batch of your favorite pie crust or store-bought pie crust
4 pounds sweet onions; cut into 1/4-inch wedges
1/4 cup olive oil
Salt and pepper to taste

Handful of pitted cured Kalamata olives; cut in half
6 or 8 anchovy fillets; chopped
1/4 pound precooked, breaded, and fried fish fillet (haddock, cod or flounder)

A pie filled with onions, olives, fish, and anchovies.

Sauté your onions in olive oil over medium heat, and add the salt and pepper to taste to the onions. Cook until golden brown, but be careful not to burn them. When the onions are completely reduced, put them in a colander with a bowl to drain as much oil out as you can. When the onions are drained and cooled, line a 9-inch pie pan with a pie crust and add the onions to the pan. Take the cured olives and spread evenly over onions, then evenly spread anchovies over the onions and olives. Break up the fish fillet into bite-size pieces, and spread evenly over the top. Cover the pie with another crust, trim the pie, pinch together, and cut some vents in the top. Bake in a preheated oven at 375 degrees for 40 minutes or until the crust is golden brown. Cover the pie crust with foil after about 30 minutes if browning too much. Serve this pie warm or room temperature. This pie even tastes better the next day.

Yield: 6 to 8 servings | Recipe by Mark Senecal

Parmesan Risotto

Serve with our Osso Buco on page 83.

1½ quarts chicken stock; heated
2 tablespoons olive oil
1 medium onion; finely minced
1½ cups arborio rice
1/2 cup dry white wine

3 tablespoons butter
1/3 cup heavy cream
1/2 cup Parmesan cheese plus extra for garnish; grated
Truffle oil for drizzling; optional

In a 3-quart saucepan on medium heat, bring the chicken broth to a simmer and turn the heat to low. In a heavy, wide-based saucepan, heat olive oil, then add onions, and cook until golden over medium heat. Add rice and stir to coat each and every grain with oil. Add the wine, and cook until it has evaporated. Begin by adding 1 cup of hot stock, stirring with a wooden spoon to mix. Allow this liquid to be absorbed, then add 1/2 cup stock, stirring until evaporated. Continue to add broth by 1/2 cupfuls, stirring after each addition. Continue until rice begins to soften. Last addition of stock should just absorb into rice, leaving it slightly tight. Stirring quickly with a wooden spoon, add butter and cream. Risotto will become very creamy. Stir in the cheese, then remove from heat and adjust seasoning to taste. Serve topped with freshly grated cheese, and drizzle with truffle oil, if using.

Yield: 4 servings | Recipe by Chef Bo

Polenta

4 cups water
1 teaspoon fine salt
1 cup polenta
3 tablespoons butter; divided
1/2 cup Parmigiano-Reggiano cheese plus more for garnish; freshly grated

Bring water and salt to a boil in a large saucepan. Slowly pour polenta into boiling water, whisking constantly until all polenta is stirred in and there are no lumps. Reduce heat to low, and simmer while whisking often until polenta starts to thicken for about 5 minutes. Polenta mixture should still be slightly loose. Cover and cook for 30 minutes, whisking every 5 to 6 minutes. When polenta is too thick to whisk, stir with a wooden spoon. Polenta is done when texture is creamy and the individual grains are tender. Turn off heat, and gently stir 2 tablespoons of butter into polenta until butter partially melts. Mix 1/2 cup Parmigiano-Reggiano cheese into polenta until cheese has melted. Cover and let stand 5 minutes to thicken. Stir and taste for salt before transferring to a serving bowl. Top polenta with remaining 1 tablespoon butter and about 1 tablespoon freshly grated Parmigiano-Reggiano cheese for garnish.

Yield: 1 quart | Recipe by Chef Bo

Polenta is nothing more than coarsely ground cornmeal. The classic ratio is 1 part polenta to 4 parts water, but I like to measure the polenta just a little scant of a full cup. Use chicken broth instead of water. It's a perfect base for any kind of saucy meat or mushroom ragout.

Parmesean Dauphinoise Potatoes

2½ pounds medium red potatoes or small bakers; peeled
2 cups heavy cream
1 cup whole milk
4 large cloves garlic; grated or thinly sliced
2 egg yolks

5 sprigs thyme; optional
1 teaspoon salt
½ teaspoon black pepper
1 cup Parmesan cheese; grated

Preheat oven to 425 degrees. You will need a well-greased 3-quart baking dish. Use a mandoline to slice the potatoes very thin. If you do not have a mandoline, use a very sharp chef's knife and slice into 1/8-inch-thick pieces. Add heavy cream, milk, garlic, egg yolks, thyme (optional), and salt and pepper to a large sauce pot and whisk together. Slowly bring the mixture to a simmer on medium heat. After mixture comes to a simmer, remove the thyme stems from the pot if used. Mix in the cheese, and whisk. Add the thin sliced potatoes to the pot, let mixture come back to a simmer, and simmer for 5 to 8 minutes. Remove pan from stove using a slotted spoon to add the potatoes to the baking dish; spoon the rest of the sauce over the potatoes. Place the baking dish on a large sheet pan and place in the oven. Bake until the dish becomes bubbly and the potatoes are easily pierced with a knife, about 35 to 40 minutes.

Yield: 8 servings | Recipe by Chef Bo

Sausage and Sage Cornbread Stuffing

2 (6.5 ounces) packages dry cornbread mix
6 cups dry seasoned bread cubes
3/4 cup butter or margarine
1 pound Ferrara's mild or sweet loose sausage
1 cup onion; chopped
1½ cups celery; chopped
6 cups chicken broth

1/2 cup fresh parsley; chopped
1 tablespoon poultry seasoning
3 tablespoons sage; freshly chopped or
   1-1/2 teaspoons dried sage
1 teaspoon salt
1 cup water or broth; optional
1/2 cup Parmesan cheese

Perfect for your Holiday feast.

Prepare the cornbread according to package instructions. Once cornbread is cooled, crumble it into a large bowl, add the bread cubes, and set aside. Add the butter to a saucepan, then add the sausage, onion, and celery, and cook until sausage is done. Add broth, parsley, poultry seasoning, sage and salt to the pan, and bring to a boil. Let simmer for 4 to 5 minutes. Add the liquid slowly while stirring the cornbread and bread cubes, making sure not to make the stuffing too wet. If the stuffing is too dry, add a little water. Add the Parmesan, and mix. Transfer to a 9x13-inch pan, or use to stuff your turkey. If in a 9x13 pan, bake covered in a preheated 350-degree oven for 40 minutes.

Yield: 8 to 10 servings | Recipe by Chef Bo

Sicilian Meatballs with Raisins

10 ounces of a good Italian bread; diced small
10 ounces water
1½ pounds 80/20 or better ground beef
1 pound of my mild sausage
4 or 5 garlic cloves; chopped
3 tablespoons parsley
1 teaspoon basil
1 teaspoon salt

1/2 teaspoon black pepper
2 ounces Parmesan or Romano cheese
4 to 6 ounces golden raisins
3 eggs; beaten
Wet bread
12 to 18 ounces of good Italian seasoned
breadcrumbs (Vigo works well)

In a bowl, add the diced bread and water together, and mix by squeezing as you incorporate the water in the bread. Set aside. The bread should be wet but at the same time hold the water. Before adding, drain off any unabsorbed water. In a large bowl, mix the beef and sausage together. Add garlic, parsley, basil, salt, pepper, cheese, raisins, and eggs. Mix everything together. Add the wet bread, and mix again. Add the dry Italian breadcrumbs 6 ounces at a time, and mix the crumbs in each time until the mixture has the right consistency. You will find what is right for you. Roll out your meatballs the size you want them to be. If you are going to fry the meatballs, add about a 1/4 inch of oil to your frying pan, and fry on a medium-high heat. Just add a few meatballs to the pan at a time, and keep rolling them to evenly brown on all sides. You can add the meatballs to your sauce to finish cooking or bake them at 325 degrees for 15 to 20 minutes. If not frying, bake them in a 350-degree preheated oven for 20 to 25 minutes. The meatballs should be added to your sauce for the last 20 to 30 minutes of the cooking time.

Yield: about 30 meatballs depending on size | Recipe by Ann Ferrara

Sandwiches & More

Fried Sausage, Peppers, Potatoes & Eggs

3/4 cup olive or vegetable oil
3 pounds red potatoes; unpeeled half-moon slices
1½ pounds mild or sweet Ferrara's Sausage; loose
   and crumbled or links cut in 1/2 inches slices
3 teaspoons garlic; chopped
1 medium onion; sliced
1 large red pepper; sliced

1 large green pepper; sliced
8 to 10 eggs
1/4 teaspoon pepper
1/2 teaspoon salt
1/4 cup Parmesan cheese
2 cups mozzarella; shredded

Add the oil to a large nonstick frying pan; heat the oil, and add the potatoes carefully; fry until they start to brown. Add the sausage to the potatoes and fry the potatoes and sausage together while stirring for 8 to 10 minutes. Add garlic, onions, and peppers, and continue to fry and stir until potatoes are done. Remove the potatoes, sausage, and vegetables from the pan, and carefully pour off all the oil. In a medium bowl, beat the eggs, add a little of the Parmesan cheese, salt and pepper, and mix. In another small bowl, mix the Parmesan and mozzarella cheese together. Reheat your pan until hot. Add your potatoes, sausage, and vegetables back to the hot pan. Wait until you can hear it start to sizzle. Add your eggs, and stir fast as your eggs scramble through the mixture. Do not overcook the eggs. Remove the mixture immediately from pan, and place on a platter. Cover with the cheese mixture and place under the broiler to melt the cheese, and do not walk away.

Yield: 4 dinners or 6 sandwiches | Recipe by Chef Bo

Italian Grilled Cheese

8 slices Italian bread
4 tablespoons butter; softened
4 ounces sun-dried tomato pesto
8 ounces fontina or Gruyere cheese; sliced

You can make this with my sun-dried tomato pesto Pastika. You can also add one or more of these: sliced tomatoes, thinly sliced prosciutto, chicken, or Genoa salami.

Spread one side of each slice of bread with butter, then flip over and lightly spread the pesto evenly over the other side of each slice. Heat your panini press, large nonstick pan, or cast-iron pan over medium heat. Place 4 slices of bread, butter side down, in the pan. Divide the cheese evenly over the bread, then top the sandwiches with the remaining bread. Cook in your press until the sandwich is golden brown and the cheese is runny. If in a pan, cook for a few minutes until the first side is golden brown. Carefully flip the sandwiches, and cook for a few more minutes until the cheese is fully melted and the bread is golden brown. Let cool slightly, then slice the sandwiches in half and serve.

Yield: 4 sandwiches | Recipe by Chef Bo

Simmered Red Wine Boston Pork

This simmered pork is great to be served as a sandwich, or over your favorite pasta or garlic mashed potatoes.

6 to 8 pounds bone in pork butt
6 to 8 garlic cloves; chopped
2 medium onions; diced
1½ cups dry red wine
1 (28 ounces) can crushed tomatoes
2 (6 ounces) cans tomato paste
28 ounces fire-roasted red peppers; sliced

3 teaspoons salt
3 teaspoons black pepper
1/4 cup ground fennel seed
1/4 cup basil
1/2 cup parsley
1/2 cup water if needed

Place the pork butt in a large Dutch oven or a slow cooker, both with a lid. In a 4-quart saucepan on medium heat, sauté the garlic and onion until light brown. Add in the wine, and reduce by 1/2. Reduce heat to a low simmer, add the crushed tomato, tomato paste, red peppers, salt, pepper, fennel, basil, and parsley, and stir the sauce till smooth. Sauce will be thick. Simmer the sauce on low for 8 to 10 minutes. If sauce is too thick, add water only as needed. Preheat oven to 275 degrees, or set the slow cooker on low. Pour the sauce over the pork butt, and cover. Cook in the oven (Dutch oven) for 4 to 4½ hours until tender, or cook in the slow cooker for 8 hours or until tender. When done, ladle off most of the grease, carefully pour or ladle off the sauce into a 3-quart saucepan, and reduce to thicken. While the sauce is reducing, pull apart the pork butt, pull out the bone, and keep the pork warm. When sauce is thickened, pour back over the pork, and mix the pork and sauce together.

Yield: 12 servings | Recipe by Chef Bo

Spicy Sausage and Red Wine Stew

3 tablespoons extra-virgin olive oil
2 pounds Ferrara's hot or mild Italian sausage
6 garlic cloves; chopped
2 red bell peppers; sliced
1 green pepper; sliced
1 large yellow onion; sliced
12 ounces mushrooms; sliced
1½ cups red wine

3 cups marinara (recipe on page 28)
1/2 teaspoon kosher salt
1/2 teaspoon freshly ground black pepper
1/4 teaspoon red pepper flakes; optional
1/2 cup Parmesan cheese
6 to 8 fresh French or crusty style rolls
8 ounces mozzarella; optional
1 pound of pasta; optional

This recipe can be served as a sandwich and is also delicious served over pasta. Choose a nice crusty roll that will hold the stew.

Heat the oil in a heavy large 4-to-6 quart skillet over medium heat. Add the raw sausage, cut in 1-inch slices, and cook until light brown for about 10 minutes, stirring as browning. Keeping the pan over medium heat, add the garlic, peppers, onions, and mushrooms. Sauté for about 5 to 8 minutes while scraping the bottom of the pan with a wooden spoon to release all the browned bits. Add the wine, and reduce by half. Add the marinara, and bring to a simmer. Add the salt, pepper, and the red pepper flakes if using. Continue simmering until the sauce has thickened, about 15 more minutes. Split the rolls in half lengthwise, and hollow out the bread from the bottom side of each roll, if nice and crusty, being careful not to puncture the crust. Fill the bottom half of the roll with the sausage mixture. Sprinkle with Parmesan cheese cover with the top half of the roll, and serve sandwiches immediately. You can also cover the filled bottom half of the roll with Parmesan and mozzarella cheese, and bake at 375 degrees until the mozzarella is melted. Now you can eat the sandwich as an open face with a knife and fork. This recipe is also delicious served over pasta.

Yield: 6 to 8 servings | Recipe by Chef Bo

Veal and Peppers

1/3 cup flour seasoned with salt and pepper to taste
4 tablespoons olive oil
2 pounds veal shoulder or stew meat;
    trimmed and cut into 1-inch cubes
Olive oil if needed
2 to 3 cloves of garlic; minced
1 cup good dry red wine
2 (28 ounces) cans crushed tomatoes
3 tablespoons tomato paste
1½ cups of water from rinsing the cans
1 medium onion; chopped
3 cups green peppers; julienned
1½ cups mushrooms; sliced; optional
1/4 cup chopped parsley
Pinch of basil
1/2 teaspoon salt
1/4 teaspoon black pepper

Combine flour, salt, and pepper together, and toss with the veal cubes. Add oil to a 4-quart saucepan, and lightly brown the veal on medium heat; remove the veal cubes before adding more oil if the pot appears too dry. Add the garlic, and cook about one minute. Add the wine to deglaze the pan, being sure to scrape up all the browned bits. Add the veal back to the pan, bring to a boil, and reduce wine by half. Add the tomatoes, pasta, and water to the pan, then cover and simmer slowly for about 20 minutes. Add the onions, peppers, mushrooms, parsley, basil, salt, and pepper. Cover and simmer for about 30 minutes or until the veal is tender. Serve over pasta, rice, or mashed potatoes. Makes a wonderful veal and pepper sandwich also.

Yield: 4 dinners or 6 sandwiches | Recipe by Chef Bo

White Wine Simmered Chicken

6 pounds boneless white and dark chicken
1/4 cup olive oil
4 garlic cloves; chopped
1 large onion; diced
1 cup dry white wine
1 (28 ounces) can crushed tomatoes
1 (6 ounces) can tomato paste
12-24 ounces roasted red peppers;
    diced or sliced

2 teaspoons salt
2 teaspoons black pepper
1 teaspoon basil
1 teaspoon oregano
2 teaspoons parsley
1/2 cup water
2 ounces Romano cheese: optional

Rinse the chicken, and place in a large Dutch oven or a slow cooker, both with a lid. In a 3-quart saucepan on medium heat, add the oil and sauté the garlic and onions until light brown. Add in the wine, and reduce by 1/2. Reduce heat to a low simmer. Add the crushed tomatoes, tomato paste, red peppers, salt, pepper, basil, oregano, and parsley, and whip sauce until smooth. Sauce will be thick. Simmer the sauce on low for 8 to 10 minutes. If sauce is too thick, add water only as needed. Preheat oven to 275 degrees, or set the slow cooker on low. Pour the sauce over the chicken, and cover. Cook in the oven for 4 to 4½ hours until tender, or cook in the slow cooker for 7 to 8 hours until tender. When done, carefully pour or ladle off the sauce into a 3-quart saucepan and reduce to thicken. While the sauce is reducing, pull apart the chicken and keep warm. When sauce is thickened, mix in Romano cheese if using, pour sauce back over the chicken, and mix the chicken and sauce together. The chicken is now ready to make simmered chicken sandwiches or to top your favorite pasta or mashed garlic potatoes.

Yield: 8 servings | Recipe by Chef Bo

This simmered chicken is great served as a sandwich, over your favorite pasta, or over garlic mashed potatoes. Choose a nice crusty-style roll that will hold the stew.

Time for Dinner

Baked Chicken Mushroom Marsala

6 boneless chicken breasts; pressed or lightly pounded
1/2 cup of flour seasoned with salt & pepper
1/4 cup oil
1 quart Marsala sauce

Preheat the oven to 325 degrees. To prepare the chicken, coat each breast with the seasoned flour. Add the oil to a 10-to-12 inch skillet, bring the oil to a medium heat, and add the chicken 3 breasts at a time. Sauté for about 5 minutes on each side or until golden brown. Remove and place on a plate until all 6 are browned. Layer the chicken breasts in a 9x12 casserole pan with a lid. Pour enough of the warm mushroom sauce over the chicken breasts to completely cover them. Place the lid on the pan, and bake for 25 to 35 minutes or until the chicken breasts are tender. Serve over pasta or rice.

Yield: 6 servings | Recipe by Chef Bo

Baked Ziti

1½ pounds ziti
2 teaspoons olive oil
3 teaspoons garlic; chopped
16 ounces lean ground beef
16 ounces Ferrara mild pork sausage;
   casing removed
1/4 cup parsley
1 teaspoon salt
1/2 cup Parmesan cheese
2 pounds whole milk ricotta cheese

1/2 cup grated Parmesan cheese
3 large eggs
2 tablespoons fresh parsley
1 tablespoon black pepper
20 ounces shredded mozzarella
1 cup grated Parmesan cheese
3 to 4 cups marinara or to taste
2 cups marinara
1/4 cup Parmesan cheese
1/2 pound mozzarella cheese for topping
1 quart sauce for serving

Make marinara sauce first. Recipe is in this book on page 28.

Preheat oven to 350 degrees. Heat oil in large saucepan or skillet over medium heat. Add the garlic, beef, sausage, parsley, and salt, and cook until just done and drain off just 75 to 80 percent of the grease. Note: Leaving in some of the grease adds flavor. Stir in 1/2 cup of the Parmesan in the meat, and keep warm.

For the cheese mix: In a medium bowl, combine ricotta, Parmesan, eggs, parsley, and pepper, and mix well. Cook ziti in large pot of boiling salted water al dente and drain well. In a large bowl, combine the hot ziti, seasoned meat, cheese mix, mozzarella, third-listed Parmesan cheese, and the 3 cups marinara, and mix everything together. Pour the ziti mixture in a 15x10½ casserole dish.

For the topping: Spread the second-listed marinara over the ziti mixture. Mix the Parmesan and mozzarella cheese together, and sprinkle the cheese mix evenly over the marinara. Cover baking dish with aluminum foil. Bake at 350 degrees for 45 minutes.

Yield: 8 to 12 servings | Recipe by Chef Bo

Black Coffee Baked Ham

1 fully cooked ham; bone-in (18 to 20 pounds)
1/2 ounce whole cloves
1 cup brown sugar
8 ounces warm black coffee
8 ounces Canada Dry Ginger Ale (room temperature)
3 cups brown sugar
1/2 cup spicy brown mustard
16 ounces black coffee
16 ounces Canada Dry Ginger Ale

Preheat the oven to 325 degrees. Score the surface of the ham about 1/8 inch deep in a diamond pattern. Insert a clove into the middle of each diamond. Mix first-listed brown sugar, coffee, and ginger ale together, then pour over the ham. Bake the ham covered for 1½ hours. While the ham is cooking, heat the remaining brown sugar, mustard, coffee, and ginger ale in a 3-quart saucepan on medium low to reduce for about 15 minutes to help thicken the glaze. After the 1½ hours, pull out the ham. Brush the glaze on the ham, and continue baking for 30 minutes, brushing the ham with the glaze every 10 minutes for the next 30 minutes of baking time or until nice and glossy.

Yield: 12 to 15 servings | Recipe by Chef Frank (Noses) Capone

Bo's Cheese-Filled Ravioli

Filling:
1 pint good ricotta cheese
8 ounces mozzarella cheese; shredded
3/4 cup imported Parmesan or
    Romano cheese; grated
1 egg
2 teaspoons fresh parsley
1/4 teaspoon salt
1/2 teaspoon black pepper

Ravioli dough: You will need an electric mixer with a
    dough hook and a pasta rolling machine.
2 cups all-purpose flour; more for dusting
1 teaspoon salt
3 large eggs
2 tablespoons extra-virgin olive oil
1 egg for egg wash
1/2 cup or more of cornmeal for dusting

To make the filling: In a large bowl, combine ricotta, mozzarella, grated cheese, egg, parsley, salt, and pepper. Mix well, and refrigerate. To make the pasta dough: Use an electric mixer fitted with a dough hook. Combine the flour and salt, add the eggs 1 at a time, and continue to mix. Drizzle in 1 tablespoon of olive oil, and keep mixing until the dough forms a ball. Sprinkle some flour on your work surface, knead, and fold the dough until it becomes elastic and smooth. This should take about 10 minutes. Form the dough into a ball, rub the dough with the remaining olive oil, and wrap the dough in plastic wrap. Let rest for about 30 minutes to let the dough relax. Cut the dough ball in 1/2, and cover the other 1/2 to prevent it from drying out. Dust your counter and the dough with a little flour. Press the dough into a rectangle shape, and roll it through your pasta machine 2 or 3 times at the widest setting. Pull and stretch the sheet of dough with the palm of your hand as it emerges from the rollers. Reduce the setting, and run through 2 or 3 times again. Continue tightening until the machine is at the narrowest setting. The dough should be about paper-thin, about 1/8-inch thick, and see-through. Dust with flour as needed.

Beat 1 egg with 1 tablespoon of water to make an egg wash. Dust the counter and the sheet of dough with flour, lay out the sheet of dough, and brush the top with the egg wash. This will act as a glue. Drop tablespoons of filling on 1/2 of the pasta sheet, about 2 inches apart. Fold the other 1/2 over the filling like a blanket. With an espresso cup or your fingers, gently press out the air pockets around each mound of filling. Use a cutter or sharp knife to cut each mound into squares, and crimp the 4 edges with a fork to make a tight seal. Dust a sheet pan and the ravioli with the cornmeal to prevent the pasta from sticking, and lay them out to dry slightly while you assemble the rest. Cook the ravioli in large pot of salted water for about 4 minutes. They'll float to the top when cooked. Remove from the pot with slotted spoon. Serve with your favorite sauce. Yield: 24 | Recipe by Chef Bo

Broccoli and Orecchiette with Sausage

Growing up, my Grandmother used to make this pasta by hand. She would dry the pasta on clean white sheets on our tables and even on beds. Today you can find orecchiette in the grocery store. My mother made this dish as a side, but I add the sausage to make it a meal.

1 pound cooked Ferrara's sausage in links; sliced in bite-size pieces (mild or sweet)
1 head of broccoli; separated into florets. Stems can be cut into bite-size pieces OR
1 large package of frozen broccoli
1 large package frozen broccoli; optional
1 pound orecchiette (save a cup of the pasta water)
3 garlic cloves; chopped fine
1/4 cup olive oil
1/2 teaspoon dried red pepper flakes or to taste
1/2 cup Parmesan cheese; grated
Salt and pepper to taste
1 tablespoon fresh parsley or 1 teaspoon dried

Grill or fry the sausage. Steam or blanch the broccoli, but don't overcook. You can also use a package of frozen broccoli and only cook until tender. It will be added to the pasta pot during the last couple of minutes of cooking time. Cook pasta in a large pot of salted boiling water for about 8 to 10 minutes or until al dente. While pasta is cooking, add the garlic and a few tablespoons of the oil in a small fry pan and lightly brown for about a minute or two. Add hot pepper flakes, stir for a minute, and set aside. Just before pasta is done, add the cooked broccoli to the boiling pasta pot. Drain, saving one cup of water, and return the pasta and broccoli back to the hot pot. Put the pasta pot back on the stove on medium heat. Add the cooked sausage, garlic, and hot pepper oil to the pot with the pasta and broccoli. Now add the cheese and the rest of the oil. Slowly add some of the reserved pasta water, and stir until a thin sauce forms. Add salt and pepper to taste. Place in serving bowl, and sprinkle with parsley.

Yield: 6 Servings | Recipe by Peggy Degearo Senecal

Cheese Manicotti

Make marinara sauce first. Recipe included in this book on page 28.

1 cup milk
2 eggs
Just less than a 1/4 cup oil
1/2 tablespoon salt
1½ cups flour
1/2 stick butter; melted
1 pint of good ricotta cheese
8 ounces mozzarella cheese; shredded

3/4 cup grated Parmesan or Romano cheese
2 teaspoons fresh parsley
1/4 teaspoon salt
1/2 teaspoon black pepper
About 3 cups of sauce
1/4 cup grated cheese for topping
2 teaspoons butter for topping

Crepe: Whip the first 5 ingredients together until smooth. In a 9½ inch preheated nonstick frying pan, add about 2 ounces of batter in the pan while rolling pan to make a nice round crepe. Cook the batter on med-low until top looks about 75% cooked, and slide out of the pan on parchment paper. Brush with butter each time and repeat process until all the batter is gone (should make about 16). Preheat oven to 350 degrees.

Filling: In a large bowl, combine ricotta, mozzarella, grated cheese, eggs, parsley, salt, and pepper. Mix well. Place 3 or 4 tablespoons of the cheese mixture on each crepe off-centered, and roll all of them up. Ladle about one cup of sauce in the bottom of a 15x10 casserole pan, place the filled crepes in the pan side by side, and cover lightly with sauce. Sprinkle with grated cheese, and dot with butter. Bake for 35 to 40 minutes, or until bubbly.

Yield: 8 servings | Recipe by Chef Bo

Chicken in Hunter Sauce (Cacciatore)

3/4 cup flour
6 boneless chicken breasts or 8 to 10 boneless chicken thighs; cut into 1½-inch-size pieces
1/4 cup olive oil
4 cloves garlic; chopped
2 onions; chopped
16 ounces mushroom; sliced
3/4 cup dry white wine
3/4 cup chicken stock
1 (28 ounce) can crushed tomatoes
1 cup water
2 teaspoons parsley
2 teaspoons salt
1 teaspoon black pepper
4 cups warm demi-glace: try Minor's Concentrate Demi-Glace on Amazon

Coat each chicken breast or chicken thigh with flour. Add the oil to a large saucepan, bring the oil to a medium heat, and add the chicken, 3 pieces at a time. Sauté for about 6 minutes on each side to brown. Remove and place on a plate until all are browned. Add the garlic, onion, and mushrooms to the pan, and sauté for 4 to 6 minutes. Deglaze the pan with the wine and chicken stock, reduce by half, and add chicken back into the pan. Add the tomato, water, parsley, salt and pepper, and simmer for about 20 minutes. Add the Demi-Glace, and simmer for 10 more minutes.

Yield: 6 to 8 servings | Recipe by Chef Bo

Chicken Linguine

3 to 4 chicken breasts; cut into 1½ inch cubes
2 cups flour seasoned with salt and pepper
1 cup oil
1 tablespoon fresh garlic; chopped
1 medium onion
1½ pounds mushrooms; sliced
2 medium red peppers; diced or julienned
1/2 cup white wine

3 cups chicken stock
1/2 teaspoon black pepper
1/2 teaspoon salt
1 stick butter
1 cup half-and-half
1 pound linguine
Parmesan cheese to taste

In a bowl, add flour, dredge the chicken chunks in the flour until coated, and save the remaining flour. In a 4-quart skillet or saucepan, add the oil and fry the chicken chunks until they are light golden brown. Do not put them all in at once. Remove the fried chicken, and hold them in a dish or bowl. Pour off 1/2 of the oil. Add garlic, onion, mushrooms and red peppers, and sauté for about 5 to 6 minutes on medium heat. Add the wine to deglaze the pan, and simmer 2 to 3 minutes. Add back the fried chicken, add the chicken stock, and simmer slowly for about 20 minutes or until chicken is tender. Lower the heat, add the salt and pepper, cut the butter in 4 pieces, and roll the butter in the saved flour. Stir into the simmering sauce one at a time to help thicken the sauce. Whip in one or two tablespoons of the saved flour to the cream. This will also help the sauce to thicken. Add some of the cream to the sauce as it is simmering, adding just enough cream to make the sauce creamy, or as you like it. In a large pot of salted water, cook the linguine al dente and ladle the sauce on your linguine and enjoy. You may add Parmesan cheese to the sauce or as you toss the sauce and linguine together. I like adding it to the sauce.

Yield: 4 to 6 servings | Recipe by Chef Bo

Story: Years ago, I had some friends coming over for dinner. I wanted to make something, but I did not know what. I knew they liked pasta, so I tried my new recipe on them. They loved it. They named it. From then on, it was Bo make that Chicken Linguine dish.

Chicken Parmesan

Make the marinara sauce recipe in this book on page 28.

Always keep your egg mix cold; keep refrigerated until ready to use.

3 large eggs
1 tablespoon garlic; minced
2 tablespoons parsley
1/2 teaspoon basil
3 tablespoons Parmesan cheese; grated
Salt and pepper to taste
6 (5 ounce) chicken breasts; lightly pounded
1 cup flour; salt and peppered to taste
3 cups Italian seasoned breadcrumbs

3/4 cup mixed vegetable oil and olive oil for frying
4 to 6 cups marinara
1/3 cup Parmesan for first baking

FOR TOPPING
8 ounces mozzarella; shredded
1/3 cup Parmesan cheese
1 tablespoon fresh parsley; chopped

Preheat oven 350 degrees.

For the chicken: Beat together (I like to beat my egg mixtures; it helps to blend all the flavors) eggs, garlic, parsley, basil, cheese, salt, and pepper in a bowl. Place the flour and breadcrumbs for coating in separate containers. Coat each breast with seasoned flour. Dip chicken into the egg mixture, making sure to evenly coat each breast with the egg. Add the chicken into the breadcrumb mixture, pressing breasts to help evenly coat, making sure the chicken is completely coated with the breading. Heat oil in a large skillet over medium heat. It is best to brown slowly on both sides, never on high heat — this helps the chicken to be tender. Fry chicken for 3 to 4 minutes on each side until about 75% done or until lightly golden on each side. Do not overcook. Cover the bottom of a baking dish with sauce (that will allow all 6 breasts to lie flat) and sprinkle with Parmesan. Place chicken in the baking dish side by side, cover with sauce, and sprinkle with more Parmesan. Bake uncovered for 25 minutes. While chicken is baking, mix the last three topping ingredients together. When the chicken comes out, turn on the broiler. Top the chicken with the mozzarella mix, and melt under the broiler or bake until cheese is melted. I like the broiler. Do not walk away and let it burn.

Yield: 6 servings | Recipe by Chef Bo

Chicken Wellington

For the chicken:
2 tablespoons olive oil
2 tablespoons butter
8 (4 or 5 ounce) boneless skinless chicken breasts
Salt and pepper to taste
2 sheets frozen puff pastry; cut out 8 4 x 4 squares
    and thaw
1 egg; slightly beaten
1/4 cup sherry
1/2 cup peas; frouncesen and thawed under running water

For the stuffing: You will need 4 cups or more of panko breadcrumbs and to make my sherry cream of mushroom soup, the recipe is in this book on page 43.

Spilt the soup in half, and let cool. You will need half the soup for the stuffing. You will use the other half of the soup as your sauce.

Here is a classic dish with my twist. You will need to make the mushroom with sherry soup (on page 43) first ~ best if made the day before.

Add your breadcrumbs slowly to one half of the soup to make a stuffing. The stuffing should still be moist. Do not make the stuffing too dry. Add more chicken stock if too dry. Heat olive oil and butter in a large skillet over medium heat. Season chicken breasts with salt and black pepper. Cook chicken in the oil until lightly golden but not cooked through, about 3 minutes per side. Transfer to a plate. Preheat oven to 350 degrees. Line a baking pan with parchment paper. Roll out each puff pastry square on about a 5x5 squared floured work surface. Place about 3 tablespoons of stuffing down on the center of each square. Place a chicken breast top side down on top of the stuffing in the center of each square, and press the chicken breast down lightly. Repeat the process for the other chicken breasts. Brush the edges of each square with water, wrap puff pastry up and around the chicken, and bring together at the top. Place seam-side down on a lined baking pan, and brush the tops with the beaten egg. Bake in the preheated oven until Wellingtons are puffed and golden brown, about 20 to 30 minutes. As the Wellingtons are cooking, purée the remaining soup and heat. Add the sherry and peas, and simmer, turning the remaining soup into a sauce. When the Wellingtons are done, ladle some of the sauce on a plate, place the wellington on the sauce, and serve. Pairs well with broccoli, carrots or green beans.

Yield: 8 servings | Recipe by Chef Bo

Eggplant Rollatini

4 medium eggplants; washed, peeled and
    sliced between 1/8 and 1/4 inch thick
1½ cups all-purpose flour
1/4 teaspoon salt
1/4 teaspoon black pepper
8 large eggs
4 to 8 garlic cloves; chopped
3 tablespoons dried parsley
1 tablespoon dried basil
1/4 teaspoon salt
1/4 teaspoon black pepper
1/3 cup Romano; grated
Vegetable oil for frying as needed
    (about 1½ to 2 cups)

Filling:
2 pounds whole milk ricotta
8 ounces mozzarella; shredded
1/2 cup imported Parmesan or Romano
    cheese; grated
2 eggs
3 teaspoons parsley
1 teaspoon basil
1/4 teaspoon salt
1/4 teaspoon black pepper
About 6 cups of marinara sauce (page 28)

Preheat oven 350 degrees.

Eggplant: Put the flour in a medium bowl, and season with first-listed salt and pepper. In another bowl, beat together (I find beating my egg mixture helps blend the flavors better) the eggs and the next 6 ingredients. Dip each eggplant slice in the flour, and shake off any excess. Then, dip in the egg mixture, and place in a container. In a large skillet, pour enough oil to accumulate about 1/2-inch in the bottom. Heat the oil to medium to fry the eggplant. Use a pair of kitchen tongs to add a single layer of the eggplant to the pan. Cook them until they are lightly brown on both sides, remove from the oil, and transfer to a baking sheet fitted with a towel so the eggplant can drain as the others cook. Take care to reheat the oil back up to temperature before adding another batch to the pan. Lay each fried eggplant out flat.

Filling: Mix all 8 ingredients until smooth, place 2½ tablespoons of filling at the wide end, and roll up, arranging them side by side in a 13x9 casserole dish. Generously ladle the sauce over the eggplant until covered. Sprinkle with grated cheese. Bake uncovered for 25 to 30 minutes.

Yield: 8 to 10 servings | Recipe by Chef Bo

Eggplant Romano

2 quarts of marinara sauce (page 28)
4 medium eggplants; washed and sliced
  between 1/8 and 1/4 inch thick; about 2½ pounds
1½ cups all-purpose flour
1/4 teaspoon salt
1/4 teaspoon black pepper
8 large eggs
4 to 8 garlic cloves; chopped
3 tablespoons dried parsley
1 tablespoon dried basil

1/4 teaspoon salt
1/4 teaspoon black pepper
1/3 cup Romano; grated
1½ to 2 cups vegetable oil for frying
1 cup Romano cheese; make sure you use
  all the Romano cheese in the assembly;
  the more the tastier
Black pepper shaker
1 pound mozzarella

Make marinara sauce first. Recipe is in this book on page 28. Always keep your egg mix cold, and keep refrigerated until ready to use.

Put the flour in a medium bowl, and season with first-listed salt and pepper. In another bowl, beat together (I find beating my egg mixture helps blend the flavors better) the eggs and the next 6 ingredients. Dip each eggplant slice in the flour, and shake off any excess. Then dip in the egg mixture, and place in a container. In a large skillet, pour enough oil to accumulate about 1/2 an inch in the bottom. Heat the oil to medium to fry the eggplant, and use a pair of kitchen tongs to add a single layer of the eggplant to the pan. Cook them until they are lightly brown on both sides, remove from the oil, and transfer to a baking sheet fitted with a towel so the eggplant can drain as the others cook. Take care to reheat the oil back up to temperature before adding another batch to the pan. Try to keep the oil from overheating and not to over-brown the eggplant. Preheat oven to 350 degrees.

To assemble: In a 9x13 baking dish, spoon enough sauce to cover the bottom of the pan, and sprinkle with cheese. Top with a layer of the fried eggplant; the eggplant slices can overlap slightly. Cover with sauce, and sprinkle generously with cheese. Shake the black pepper lightly on every other layer. Repeat the layering until the pan is full, then top with sauce and cheese. Once assembled, cover with foil (can also be baked uncovered) place the dish in the preheated oven, and cook for 40 minutes. You can now cover with mozzarella cheese if you'd like and put the dish under the broiler for a minute or two to melt. Do not get distracted since the cheese will burn fast.

Yield: 6 to 8 servings | Recipe by Chef Bo

Fennel Sauce with Chicken

1/4 cup olive oil
1/2 a fresh fennel frond; sliced
1 medium onion; sliced
2 garlic cloves; minced
4 to 5 medium boneless skinless chicken breasts; largely diced
1½ cups chicken stock

1 (28 ounces) can crushed tomatoes
1/2 cup anisette
2 bay leaves
1 teaspoon salt
1/4 teaspoon pepper
1 pound penne

In large saucepan on medium heat, add the oil, and sauté fennel, onion, and garlic until onions are translucent. Add the chicken, and cook 4 to 5 minutes longer. Add stock, tomatoes, anisette, bay leaves, salt, and pepper. Bring to boil over medium high heat. After mixture boils, reduce heat to low, cover, and simmer for 20 to 25 minutes. Cook penne al dente in a large pot of salted water. Drain, and toss with sauce.

Yield: 4 to 6 servings | Recipe by Chef Bo

Guinness Pot Roast

3 pounds chuck roast
3 tablespoons all-purpose flour
2 teaspoons oil
2 onions; sliced
12 ounces mushrooms; sliced; optional
2 garlic cloves; minced
2 cups large carrots; sliced

8 red potatoes; quartered
Salt and pepper to taste
1 (28 ounces) can diced plum tomatoes
2 teaspoons tomato paste
3 cups beef stock
1/4 cup parsley; chopped
1 (12 ounce) can of Guinness beer

Serve with a crusty French baguette or a good artisan Italian bread. You can carefully remove the meat, put the Dutch oven on a burner, and thicken the sauce if needed.

Preheat oven 300 degrees. Season meat with salt and pepper, and coat with flour. In a large nonstick 5-quart Dutch oven, heat oil over medium-high heat, add beef, and sear the meat on all sides until brown. Remove the meat, add onions and mushrooms to the pot, and sauté for 6 minutes. Add garlic, and sauté for 2 minutes, continually stirring. Add the meat back to the pot, then cover the meat with the carrots, potatoes, salt, and pepper. In a large bowl, mix the tomatoes, tomato paste, beef stock, parsley, and beer together. Pour the mixture over the vegetables and meat. Put the cover on the Dutch oven, and put in the oven. Bake for 3 hours.

Yield: 6 to 8 servings | Recipe by Moe Mahar

Homestyle Beef and Sausage Meatloaf

2 pounds ground chuck
1/2 pound sweet or mild sausage
1/2 cup chopped onion lightly sautéed
1/2 cup chopped red or green peppers
   lightly sautéed
2 tablespoons chopped fresh parsley
1 teaspoon ground garlic
1 teaspoon salt

1/2 teaspoon pepper
3 tablespoons Worcestershire sauce
1/2 cup ketchup
2 large eggs; lightly beaten
2 cups breadcrumbs; Italian seasoned or plain
1 cup ketchup
4 teaspoons brown sugar

Preheat the oven to 350 degrees. Spray a small roasting pan, or use a nonstick pan. In a large bowl, mix together the ground chuck, sausage, sauteed onions, peppers, parsley, garlic, salt, pepper, Worcestershire sauce, the first-listed ketchup, eggs, and breadcrumbs. In a small bowl, mix the second-listed ketchup and brown sugar together. Shape the meatloaf into a 10-inch-long and 6-inch-wide loaf. Place the meatloaf in the baking pan, make a 1/2 inch well down the center of the meatloaf, and fill the well with the ketchup mix or just spread evenly over the top. Bake for about 55 minutes or until a meat thermometer registers 165 degrees. Let the meatloaf stand for 10 minutes before slicing.

Yield: 6 to 8 servings | Recipe by Chef Bo

Italian Beef Stew

2 pounds chuck pot roast, cut into chunks
3 tablespoons all-purpose flour
2 teaspoons olive oil
2 onions; sliced
2 cups fresh mushrooms; sliced; optional
2 garlic cloves; minced
1 (28 ounces) can crushed tomatoes
2 teaspoons tomato pasta
3 cups water

1 to 2 cubes of beef bouillon
2 cups large carrots; sliced
6 red potatoes, quartered
2 cups fresh green beans; 1/2 inch cut
1/4 cup parsley; chopped
1 can corn; drain 1/2 the liquid
1 can peas; drain 1/2 the liquid
Salt and pepper to taste
1/4 cup parsley; chopped

Serve with crusty French bread and salad.

Season stew meat with salt and pepper, and coat beef with flour, shaking off excess. In a 6-quart saucepan, heat olive oil over medium-high heat, add beef, and sauté until brown. Add onions and mushrooms to pan, and sauté for 6 minutes. Add garlic, and sauté for 1 minute, continually stirring. Add the tomatoes, tomato paste, water, bouillon, carrots, potatoes and green beans, add enough water to cover all the vegetables, and bring to a simmer for 25 minutes. Add the parsley, corn, peas, and remaining liquid. Stir everything well, and put the top on the pot, and simmer about 15 minutes or until the beef is tender. Sprinkle with parsley when serving.

Yield: 6 to 8 servings | Recipe by Chef Bo

Italian Beef Braciole

3 pounds of 1/4 inch sliced top round of beef Sirloin; cut into long strips
8 garlic cloves; minced
1 cup Romano cheese; freshly grated
1 cup golden raisins
3/4 cup pine nuts
2 cups dried parsley
3/4 cup dried basil
6 ounces prosciutto, sliced paper thin; optional
Cotton Butcher's String (for tying the Braciole)
2 tablespoons extra-virgin olive oil

1/4 cup extra-virgin olive oil
5 cloves garlic; minced
1 medium yellow onion
2 (28 ounces) cans crushed tomatoes
1 (6 ounces) can tomato paste
About 1½ cups of water from rinsing cans
4 tablespoons parsley
1½ teaspoons basil
1 tablespoon kosher salt
1 teaspoon black pepper
Romano cheese

With a meat hammer, pound out the slices of beef until they're thinner, about 7" long x 4" wide. Cover each beef slice with garlic, Romano cheese, raisins, pine nuts, parsley, and basil (splitting everything evenly over the meat). You should not be able to see the meat when done right. Add a thin sheet of prosciutto if using. Roll up the sheet of beef, and tie each roll securely on each end and in the middle with butcher's twine. Heat two tablespoons of olive oil in a 6-quart saucepan, and brown the Braciole on all sides. Transfer to a plate. In the saucepan on medium heat, sauté in the second-listed olive oil, garlic, and onions until translucent, about 8 minutes but not burned. Add the tomatoes, tomato paste, water, and the browned Braciole. Cover the saucepan, and simmer slowly for 2 hours. Add the herbs, salt and pepper, and allow the sauce to simmer on low heat for 30 minutes, cooking it low and slow. Be sure to stir the sauce frequently so it doesn't burn on the bottom. If the sauce becomes too thick, thin it by adding a bit of water. When done, carefully remove the butcher's twine from the Braciole. Spoon some of this wonderful flavored sauce over your favorite pasta and one or two of the Braciole. Top with some Romano cheese, and enjoy!

Yield: 4 to 8 servings | Recipe by Chef Bo

Let's Cook Something Good

Joe's Pasta Puttanesca

PREP LIST
1/4 cup Italian (flat-leaf) parsley fresh, minced
1/4 cup oregano fresh, minced
1/4 cup basil fresh, minced
1 large green bell pepper cored & sliced
1 large red bell pepper cored & sliced
1 large yellow bell pepper cored & sliced
1 large white onion sliced in large wedges
1/2 cup Kalamata olives; halved and quartered
8 ounces mushrooms sliced thick
5 cloves garlic sliced thin

1/4 cup olive oil
1 (2 ounces) can anchovies in olive oil flat fillets
2 tablespoons tomato paste
1 (28 ounces) can peeled plum tomatoes;
　　roughly chopped
1/2 teaspoon dried red pepper flakes
1/4 teaspoon black pepper
1/4 cup capers, small drained
1 pound penne or ziti pasta with lines
1/2 cup grated Parmigiano-Reggiano or
　　Romano cheese

Add olive oil to a large 12-or 14-inch frying pan, and heat on medium. Add the sliced garlic and fry for about two minutes. Add anchovies and the oil, and fry for one more minute, stirring to dissolve anchovies. Stir in tomato paste, cook for two minutes, and add all the peppers. Then cover, and cook for about 5 minutes on medium-high. Add onions and mushrooms, and cook covered for about 5 minutes on medium-high. Open plum tomatoes, drain the juice into a container. Remove cover, and add tomatoes and juice, red and black pepper, olives, and capers. Reduce heat, and simmer to thicken with the cover removed. Place a pot with 4 quarts of water on the burner. When it comes to a boil, salt it and add pasta. Now add and stir in the minced herbs to the sauce, and continue to simmer the sauce while the pasta is cooking. When pasta is al dente, save a little pasta water, then drain the pasta, but don't rinse. Place pasta in a warmed serving dish. Pour sauce over pasta, and combine. Add some of the saved pasta water if necessary. Stir in grated cheese, and let the pasta absorb the sauce a minute or so before serving.

Yield: 4 to 6 servings | Recipe by Joe DeGearo

This is my favorite version of Puttanesca. Preparation time is about 1/2 hour, and cooking time is about an hour.

I prefer penne or ziti with lines instead of spaghetti. Restaurants will sometimes add meat or fish to their Puttanesca and offer it as a daily special. In my opinion, that doesn't add much to the dish as the routine ingredients are bold, hearty, and flavorful enough on their own.

No Cream Spaghetti Carbonara

1 pound spaghetti
3 to 6 ounces pancetta or bacon to taste; diced
3 tablespoons extra-virgin olive oil; divided
2 whole large eggs plus 6 yolks
1/3 cup pecorino Romano; grated

1/4 cup Parmigiano-Reggiano; grated
1 teaspoon black pepper plus more for serving;
    freshly coarse ground
1 cup frozen peas; thawed
Saved pasta water

Recipe Note: After setting mixing bowl over the pot of boiling water (double boiler), make sure your metal bowl fits it right. Make sure bottom of bowl does not touch the boiling water.

Bring a pot of salted water to a boil. Add pasta, and cook until al dente. Bring the pot of water back to a boil to use as a double boiler. Meanwhile, combine the pancetta or bacon with 2 tablespoons olive oil in a large deep skillet. Cook while stirring frequently over medium heat until the bacon is crisp, about 7 minutes. In a large metal heatproof mixing bowl, whisk together whole eggs and yolks, pecorino Romano, Parmigiano-Reggiano, and black pepper. Add cooked pasta to skillet (you can re-dip the pasta to make it hot again if needed) with crisped bacon and its fat (be sure to save the boiling pasta water). Add remaining 1 table-spoon olive oil to pasta, stir to combine, and let cool slightly. Scrape the pasta, bacon, and all the fat into the metal bowl with the egg mixture. Add 1/2 cup pasta-cooking water and peas to pasta and egg mixture. Stir well to combine. Set mixing bowl over pot of boiling pasta water, and make sure bottom of bowl does not touch the water. Cook while stirring quickly until sauce thickens to a cream. Remove from heat. Serve right away, topping with more grated cheese and freshly ground pepper as desired. Serve with salad and bread.

Yield: 4 to 6 servings | Recipe by Chef Bo

Osso Buco

4 (12 ounces) veal shanks
Kosher salt
Black pepper; freshly ground
1 cup vegetable oil
1 cup all-purpose flour
2 carrots; peeled and diced
2 celery ribs; diced
1 yellow onion; diced
6 garlic cloves; sliced

1 cup dry red
4 cups demi-glace; try Minor's Concentrate
    Demi-Glace on Amazon
3 cups canned plum tomatoes; drained and crushed
2 sprigs fresh thyme
1 sprig fresh rosemary
1 bay leaf
2 tablespoons lemon zest; grated
2 tablespoons fresh flat-leaf parsley; chopped

Serve with Parmesan Risotto. Recipe is in this book on page 50.

Preheat the oven to 325 degrees. Season the veal shanks with salt and pepper. Heat a large, oven-proof casserole dish with lid (I like using a 12-inch round that is 6 to 8 inches deep) over medium-high heat. Put the oil into the casserole dish, and let it heat. Meanwhile, put the flour in a shallow bowl, dredge the veal shanks in it, and pat off the excess. Brown the veal shanks in the hot oil for about 3 minutes on each side, or until browned on all sides. Remove from the pan, and set aside. Add the carrots, celery, onion, and garlic to the pan, and cook over medium-high heat for 3 to 5 minutes, stirring constantly. Add the wine, bring to a boil, and reduce by half and return the veal shanks to the pan. Add the demi, tomatoes, thyme, rosemary, and bay leaf to the pan, and bring to a boil over high heat. Once the liquid boils, cover, transfer to the oven, and cook for 2½ hours until the meat is fork-tender and ready to fall off the bones. Remove any large herbs from the braising liquid and discard. Remove the veal shanks, being careful not to break them up and to keep the bone in place, set aside, and keep warm. Bring cooking stock to a boil over medium-high heat, reduce the heat, and simmer for 10 to 15 minutes or until reduced by a quarter to help thicken the sauce. Using a skimmer or large spoon, skim off any grease or foam that rises to the surface. Add a serving of risotto in a bowl or plate. Place a single osso buco (veal shank) on the risotto, and ladle about 3/4 cup of the sauce and vegetables over it. Garnish each osso buco with the fresh lemon zest and chopped parsley.

Yield: 4 servings | Recipe by Chef Bo

Pastika Rib-Eye Steak & Garlic Roasted Potatoes

My Pastika is a great pairing for steak.

2 pounds small red or white potatoes
1/4 cup good olive oil
1¼ teaspoons kosher salt
3/4 teaspoon black pepper; freshly ground
4 to 6 garlic cloves; chopped
3 tablespoons parsley; freshly chopped or
   3 tablespoons Ferrara's Mild Roasted
   Red Pepper Pastika

4 to 6 cloves garlic; roughly chopped
1 tablespoon fresh basil; chopped
1 tablespoon fresh parsley; chopped
1 tablespoon kosher salt
1/2 cup olive oil
1 teaspoon pepper
4 (16 ounces) bone in beef rib-eye steaks;
   cut 1-inch thick
4 teaspoons Ferrara's hot or mild Pastika

Preheat the oven to 350 degrees.

Potatoes: Cut the potatoes in half or quarters, and place in a bowl with the olive oil, salt, pepper, and garlic. Toss until the potatoes are well coated. Transfer the potatoes to a sheet pan, and spread out into 1 layer. Roast in the oven for 40 minutes or until golden brown. Remove the potatoes from the oven, toss with the fresh chopped parsley or Ferrara's Mild Pastika, keep warm, and serve with your steaks.

For the steak: Place the garlic, basil, parsley, and salt into a small bowl. Stir in the olive oil and pepper, and mix until evenly blended. Scrape half of the mixture into a separate small bowl, and set aside. Spread the remaining half of the herb mixture evenly over the steaks, then set aside to marinate for 1 to 4 hours. Preheat your grill on medium-high heat, and lightly oil the grate. Cook the steaks on the preheated grill for 3 to 5 minutes, then turn over, and coat with the reserved herb mixture. Continue cooking 3 to 5 minutes more for medium, or until your desired degree of cooking has been reached. Take off the grill, spread one teaspoon of the Pastika evenly over each steak, and serve with garlic-roasted potatoes.

Yield: 4 servings | Recipe by Chef Bo

Pork Roast with Apple & Pear Chutney

4 to 6 pounds pork rib roast bone-in center cut
1 teaspoon fresh rosemary; chopped
3 teaspoons mustard
1/2 teaspoon salt
1/2 teaspoon cracked black pepper

4 garlic cloves; chopped
Apple & Pear Chutney; recipe on page 12
6 tablespoons olive oil; divided

Make chutney first; find recipe on page 12.

Preheat the oven to 325 degrees. Make the apple and pear chutney: In a small bowl, mix the rosemary, mustard, salt, pepper, garlic, and first-listed olive oil together. Rub the roast all over with the mixture. In a large skillet over medium-high heat, sear the roast in the remaining olive oil for about 3 to 5 minutes on each side, or until nicely browned. Searing it will keep the juices inside of the meat and yield a roast that is moist inside and crispy outside. Place the pork in a roasting pan, and roast uncovered for 1 hour and 20 minutes or until the roast registers at least 145 degrees when a meat thermometer is inserted in the thickest part of the meat. Take out of the oven, and let the roast rest for 10 minutes before slicing. You can cut between the ribs into separate chops or between every other one. Top with chutney, and enjoy.

Yield: 4 to 6 servings | Recipe by Chef Bo

Rigatoni with Vodka Sauce

6 tablespoons butter
4 garlic cloves; chopped
1 medium onion; chopped
1 cup high-quality vodka
2 (28 ounces) cans crushed tomatoes

1 can of water from rinsing the cans
2 cups (1 pint) heavy cream
3 to 4 basil leaves; chopped
2 pounds rigatoni
1/2 cup Romano cheese

In a skillet over medium heat, add the butter and sauté the garlic and onions until slightly brown and soft. Pour in vodka, and let reduce by half. Add in the crushed tomatoes and water, and simmer for 30 minutes. Add the heavy cream, basil, and simmer for another 30 minutes or until thickened. Cook the rigatoni al dente in slightly salted water. Drain and toss with the sauce, and top with Romano cheese.

Yield: 8 to 10 servings | Recipe by Chef Bo

Roasted Mustard Chicken

1 whole roasting chicken; split or cut in 8 pieces
   OR 12 chicken thighs bone in
1/4 pound Italian sausage cut in 2-inch links; optional
3 tablespoons olive oil
1/4 cup white wine
3 tablespoons garlic; mince

1/2 cup whole grain or Dijon mustard
2 pounds red potatoes; quartered
1½ pounds carrots; cut in 2-or 3-inch pieces
Salt and pepper to season
4 or 5 fresh sprigs of rosemary

Preheat oven to 350 degrees. In a small bowl, whip the oil, wine, garlic, and mustard together, and set aside. In an oversized roasting pan, add the chicken, skin side up, and add the sausage if using. Place the potatoes and carrots around the chicken, and then generously season everything with the salt, pepper, and rosemary to your taste. Paint chicken, sausage, and vegetables with the mustard mixture. Bake 1 hour, and 20 minutes, or cook until the chicken and potatoes are golden brown.

Yield: 4 to 6 servings | Recipe by Chef Bo

When roasting chicken, use an oversized roasting pan that will allow enough space for the chicken to brown.

If you use a pan that is too small, the chicken will steam instead of roast.

Sausage and Beef-Filled Cannelloni

Make marinara sauce first. Recipe is in this book on page 28. I like to serve it with a crisp green salad and warm crusty French bread. Enjoy!

PASTA CREPE
3 eggs
1½ cups milk
1/2 cup oil
1/2 tablespoon salt
1½ cups flour

BÉCHAMEL SAUCE
3 tablespoons butter
1/3 cup flour
1½ cups milk
1 cup half-and-half
Salt
1/4 teaspoon white pepper
1/4 teaspoon nutmeg; grated
1/4 cup Romano; grated
1 tablespoon butter

MEAT FILLING
3 tablespoons butter
1/2 cup small onions; diced
2 garlic cloves; chopped
3/4 pound Ferrara Sausage; out of casing
3/4 pound ground sirloin
1 large tomato; peeled and diced
8 ounces marinara; page 28 of this book
1/2 tablespoon marjoram
1/2 tablespoon parsley
3 ounces Romano cheese
1 egg; beaten
About 1/2 cup or more Italian breadcrumbs
8 ounces mozzarella cheese
1/4 cup Romano for topping

First make marinara sauce; recipe is on page 28. Preheat oven to 350 degrees. **Pasta crepe:** Whip the first 5 ingredients together until smooth. In a preheated 9½ inch nonstick frying pan, brush with butter each time. Ladle 1.75 ounces of batter in the pan, and roll pan to make a nice round crepe. Cook until top looks about 75% or more dry, and slide off pan on parchment paper. Repeat process until all the batter is gone. Should make about 18 to 20 crepes. **Meat filling:** In a large frying pan, add butter and sauté onion and garlic for 1 to 2 minutes. Add sausage and ground sirloin, and cook until just done. Add diced tomato, marinara, marjoram, and parsley, then simmer for 8 to 10 minutes. Let cool for about one hour, then add Romano cheese and egg. Add breadcrumbs until the filling holds together; it should have a raw meat-loaf consistency. If too loose, add more breadcrumbs. Reserve the mozzarella and romano for later. **Béchamel sauce:** Melt the butter in a 3-quart saucepan, add flour to make a roux, and cook 2 to 3 minutes. Add the milk and cream, and bring to a slow boil while whisking the whole time until thickened. Season to taste with salt, white pepper, and freshly grated nutmeg and Romano. To make the cannellonis, place about 2½ ounces of filling across crepe, sprinkle with mozzarella, and roll up. Repeat until all the crepes are filled. Arrange the filled crepes side by side in a single layer in an 8x13-inch casserole pan, 4 to 6 across the top of the pan, and repeat for the bottom of the pan. Cover crepe with the Béchamel sauce, dot with remaining butter, and sprinkle with remaining Romano cheese. Bake uncovered for 25 to 30 minutes until bubbling and hot. Yield: 8 to 10 servings | Recipe by Chef Bo

Let's Cook Something Good

Sausage Lasagna

3 quarts of marinara sauce
2 tablespoons olive oil
3 teaspoons garlic; chopped
20 ounces lean ground beef
12 ounces Ferrara mild pork sausage; casing removed
1/4 cup fresh parsley; chopped
1 teaspoon salt
1/2 cup Parmesan cheese
2 pounds whole milk ricotta cheese

1½ cups Parmesan cheese; grated
3 large eggs
2 tablespoons fresh parsley
1 teaspoon basil
1 tablespoon black pepper
24 cooked al dente lasagna noodles
1/4 pound mozzarella for topping noodles
2 pounds mozzarella for assembling

Make marinara sauce first. Recipe is in this book on page 28.

Preheat oven to 350 degrees.

Meat filling: Heat oil in large skillet over medium heat. Add garlic, beef, sausage, parsley, and salt, cook until just done, and drain. Stir in 1/2 cup Parmesan cheese to the meat mixture.

Cheese filling: Combine ricotta, Parmesan, eggs, parsley, basil, pepper in medium bowl, and mix.

Assemble the lasagna. Cook noodles in large pot of boiling salted water until al dente, about 10 minutes. Drain, rinse with cold water, and drain. Spread 1/2 cup sauce over bottom of 15x10 inch baking dish. Place 8 noodles over sauce, overlapping to fit. Sprinkle lightly with mozzarella, and spread half of the seasoned meat evenly over the noodles. Spoon 1½ cups of sauce over meat, and spread 1/2 of ricotta mixture evenly over the meat, spreading with spatula to cover meat. Sprinkle 1/2 of the second-listed rmozzarella cheese evenly over ricotta cheese, and repeat layering with 8 noodles. For next layer, add remaining meat, spoon 1½ cups of sauce over meat again, spread remaining ricotta mixture over meat, and sprinkle the remaining mozzarella cheese over the ricotta. Arrange remaining 8 noodles over the top, and wet the top noodles lightly with sauce. Cover baking dish with aluminum foil. Bake lasagna for 50 to 60 minutes. Best to let lasagna stand 10 minutes before cutting.

Yield: 9 to 12 servings | Recipe by Chef Bo

Steak Pizzaiola

Serve with garlic mashed potatoes.

3 pounds 7 bone beef steak; cut 1-1/4 inch thick is best, or a bone-in or boneless chuck steak; split
1 teaspoon coarse salt
Black pepper; freshly ground
2 tablespoons extra-virgin olive oil
3 to 4 garlic cloves; chopped
1 teaspoon dried oregano
Pinch of crushed red pepper flakes

1 tablespoon tomato paste
1 (28 ounces) can crushed tomatoes
1/4 cup Romano cheese; grated
2 medium onions; sliced
Optional toppings: Sliced red or green peppers, sliced mushrooms, black olives
1/4 cup Romano cheese; grated
1 pound mozzarella; shredded

Preheat the oven to 300 degrees. Season the meat on both sides with salt and pepper. Place the meat in a roasting pan about the size of the steak. In a large bowl, add the oil, garlic, oregano, red pepper flakes, tomato paste, tomatoes, and first-listed grated Romano cheese, stir everything well, and top meat with the onions and any of the other optional vegetables you are using. Spoon the sauce over the meat and vegetables until completely covered. Then cover the pan tightly, or place tin foil over the pan. Bake 1½ hours, then uncover and cook for an additional 15 minutes or until the sauce thickens. Top with the second-listed grated Romano cheese and mozzarella, and bake for 5 to 8 more minutes, or put it under a broiler to melt the cheese — do not walk away.

Yield: 4 to 6 servings | Recipe by Chef Bo

Veal Parmesan

2 large eggs
1 tablespoon garlic; minced
2 tablespoons parsley
½ teaspoon basil
3 tablespoons Parmesan cheese; grated
Salt and pepper to taste
6 (4 to 5 ounces) veal cutlets; pounded
 and tenderized
1 cup flour; salt and peppered to taste

3 cups Italian seasoned breadcrumbs
3/4 cup mixed vegetable oil and olive oil for frying
3 to 4 cups marinara; (marinara sauce on page 28)
1/3 cup Parmesan for first baking
8 ounces mozzarella; shredded
1/3 cup Parmesan cheese
1 tablespoon fresh parsley; chopped

Preheat oven 350 degrees.

For the veal: Beat together eggs, garlic, parsley, basil, cheese, salt, and pepper in a bowl (I like to beat the egg mixture; it helps to blend all the flavors). Place the flour and breadcrumbs for coating in small, shallow separate containers. Coat each cutlet with seasoned flour. Dip cutlet into the egg mixture, making sure to evenly coat each with the egg. Add the cutlets into the breadcrumb mixture, pressing to help evenly coat and making sure the cutlets are completely coated with the breading. Now the cutlets are ready to be browned. Heat 1/2 cup oil in a large skillet over medium heat. Fry each cutlet for 2 to 3 minutes on each side until about 75% done or until lightly golden on each side. Do not overcook. Cover the bottom of a baking dish (that will allow all 6 cutlets to lie flat) with sauce, and sprinkle with Parmesan. Place the veal side by side in the baking dish, cover with sauce, and sprinkle with more Parmesan. Bake uncovered for 20 minutes. While cutlets are baking, mix the last 3 topping ingredients. When the cutlets come out, turn on the broiler. Top each cutlet with the mozzarella mix, and melt under the broiler, or bake until cheese is melted (I like the broiler). Do not walk away and let it burn.

Yield: 6 servings | Recipe by Chef Bo

For the Love of Sausage

Cheese & Parsley (Shivilatz or Luganega) Pork Sausage

5 pounds boned pork butt
2½ tablespoons cracked black pepper
1½ cups chopped Italian parsley
8 ounces grated imported provolone cheese
3 ounces imported Romano cheese
1½ tablespoons kosher salt
6 to 8 feet of casings

Trim the pork, cut it into 1-inch cubes, and grind it through the coarse grind plate of your meat grinder.

Add the black pepper, parsley, cheese and salt evenly over the meat. Mix thoroughly for at least 2 minutes. Use your hands for mixing to ensure even distribution. Once the sausage is fully mixed, stuff it into casings.

This is a unique full-flavored classic sausage with no fennel or heat. This sausage can be kept in the refrigerator for 3 to 4 days or in the freezer for up to 3 months.

This has the perfect blend of imported pecorino Romano and provolone cheese with fresh chopped parsley and cracked black pepper. This sausage should set for one day before cooking.

Yield: 30 links | Recipe by Chef Bo

Chicken Sun-Dried Tomato Parmesan Sausage

2¾ pounds white meat, skin off
4¾ pounds dark meat, skin on
1½ ounces fresh chopped basil leaves
2½ tablespoons de-stemmed fresh chopped rosemary
3.5 ounces of fresh chopped garlic

2 teaspoons cracked black pepper
10 ounces chopped sun-dried tomatoes
6 ounces Parmesan cheese
2½ tablespoons salt
32-35mm natural* or collagen casing

Natural casings are pork. This sausage is known for its unique flavor with no heat.

Cut the chicken into 1-inch cubes, and grind it through the fine plate of your meat grinder. Add the spices, sun-dried tomatoes and cheese evenly over the meat.

Mix thoroughly for at least 2 minutes. Use your hands for mixing to ensure even distribution. Once the sausage is fully mixed, either stuff it into casings or make it into patties.

This sausage should be cooled as soon as it is done. This sausage should sit for one day before cooking. It can be kept in the refrigerator for 2 to 3 more days or in the freezer for up to 3 months.

Yield: 30 links | Recipe by Chef Bo

Mild or Hot Italian Sausage

5 pounds boned pork butt
3 tablespoons cracked or whole fennel seed
1½ tablespoons of crushed red pepper flakes to make it mild sausage or
    3 tablespoons of crushed red pepper flakes to make it hot sausage
1½ tablespoons kosher salt
1/4 cup ice water
32-35 mm natural or collagen casing

Trim the pork, cut it into 1-inch cubes, and grind it through the fine plate of your meat grinder.

Add the spices evenly over the meat; pour the ice water evenly over the meat.

Mix thoroughly for at least 2 minutes. Use your hands for mixing to ensure even distribution.

Once the sausage is fully mixed, either stuff it into casings or make it into patties or bulk packages.

This sausage should be cooled as soon as it is done. This sausage should sit for one day before cooking. It can be kept in the refrigerator for 2 to 3 more days or in the freezer for up to 3 months.

Yield: 30 links | Recipe by Chef Bo

Roasted Red Pepper Spice Pastika Chicken Sausage

3 pounds white meat boneless skinless
2 pounds dark meat boneless skinless
8 ounces Roasted red peppers
2 ounces garlic
2½ tablespoons red pepper seeds; more if you like

6 ounces of my mild or hot Pastika
1¼ tablespoons kosher salt
2 to 3 ounces of soy protein concentrate
32-35 mm natural or collagen casing

Cut the chicken into 1-inch cubes. Grind the chicken, roasted peppers, and garlic through the fine plate of your meat grinder.

Add the red pepper seeds, Pastika, salt and soy to the ground chicken meat.

Mix thoroughly for at least 3 minutes. Use your hands for mixing to ensure even distribution.

Once the sausage is fully mixed, either stuff it into casings or make it into patties or bulk packages.

This sausage should be cooled as soon as it is done. This sausage should sit for one day before cooking. It can be kept in the refrigerator for 2 to 3 more days or in the freezer for up to 3 months.

Yield: 30 links | Recipe by Chef Bo

Natural Casings are pork. This sausage needs a binder. The sausage comes out very loose (wet). The soy helps you to be able to fill the sausage into the casing. You can leave out the soy if you leave the sausage in the loose form.

Spicy Blend Chicken Sausage

Natural casings are pork.

2¾ pounds white meat, skin off
4¾ pounds dark meat, skin on
1 ounce paprika
2½ tablespoons garlic powder
2 tablespoons crushed red pepper

1/2 ounce cracked black pepper
1 teaspoon onion powder
1 teaspoon ground mustard
2 tablespoons salt
32-35 mm natural or collagen casing

Cut the chicken into 1-inch cubes, and grind it through the fine plate of your meat grinder. Add the spices evenly over the meat.

Mix thoroughly for at least 2 minutes. Use your hands for mixing to ensure even distribution. Once the sausage is fully mixed, either stuff it into casings or make it into patties or bulk packages.

This sausage should be cooled as soon as it is done. This sausage should sit for one day before cooking. It can be kept in the refrigerator for 2 to 3 more days or in the freezer for up to 3 months.

Yield: 30 links | Recipe by Chef Bo

Sweet Italian Sausage

5 pounds boned pork butt
3 tablespoons cracked or whole fennel seed
2½ tablespoons cracked black pepper
1½ tablespoons kosher salt
1/4 cup ice water
32-35 mm natural or collagen casing

Trim the pork, cut it into 1-inch cubes, and grind it through the fine plate of your meat grinder. Add the spices evenly over the meat and pour the ice water evenly over the meat.

Mix thoroughly for at least 2 minutes. Use your hands for mixing to ensure even distribution. Once the sausage is fully mixed, either stuff it into casings or make it into patties or bulk packages; you can also use as breakfast sausage links.

This sausage should be cooled as soon as it is done. This sausage should sit for one day before cooking. It can be kept in the refrigerator for 2 to 3 more days or in the freezer for up to 3 months.

Yield: 30 links | Recipe by Chef Bo

Sweet Endings

Almond Crescent Cookies

1/2 pound butter; room temperature
1/2 cup sugar
2 eggs
1 teaspoon almond extract
2 cups all-purpose flour
1/4 teaspoon salt
1 cup almonds; sliced or slivered
1½ cups confectioners' sugar for coating

In your mixer, cream sugar and butter for 5 minutes or more. Add eggs and almond extract, then mix until well blended. On low speed, gradually mix in flour, salt, and almonds. Mix just until blended. Wrap dough in plastic film wrap, and refrigerate for 1 to 2 hours. Preheat oven to 350 degrees, and line cookie sheets with parchment. Roll out dough into long pencil-like strips about 1/2 inch in diameter, cut the strips into 3-inch-long pieces, and bend into horseshoe shapes. Place in crescent shape on baking sheet about 1 inch apart. Bake for 18 minutes or until bottoms of cookies are just golden. While hot, gently roll each cookie (one at a time) in confectioners' sugar. Cool cookies on wire racks. Cool and store in an airtight container. The cookies freeze well.

Yield: 65 cookies | Recipe by Chef Bo

Apple Pear Pie

Pastry dough: This will make 2 double crust pies or 4 cobbler toppings

2½ cups flour
1/4 cup sugar (1/2 cup if you like it sweeter like me)
1/2 teaspoon salt
1/2 cup butter or margarine
1/4 oil
1/4 cup water
1 large egg; beaten

Apple pie filling:
3 Granny Smith apples; peeled and diced or sliced
1 pear (Bartlett or Bosc); peeled and diced or sliced
3 Northern-grown McIntosh apples; peeled and diced or sliced

1½ cups sugar
4 or 5 drops fresh lemon
1½ teaspoons cinnamon
1 or 2 dashes of nutmeg
1 or 2 dashes of salt
2 tablespoons flour or cornstarch
4 teaspoons quick-cook tapioca
3 tablespoons cold butter; sliced

To top the pie:
1/4 cup water
1/4 cup sugar

I don't know about you, but I love homemade pie. I enjoy the crust as much as the filling. You can use your favorite pie crust recipe or try my tasty pastry crust.

Preheat oven to 425 degrees. Lightly moisten a paper towel with vegetable oil, and rub it over the surface of a 10" pie dish to prevent sticking. **Dough:** In a bowl, combine flour, sugar, and salt. Cut in the butter with mixer on low until the mix turns into pea size particles, and reserve. In a large bowl, add the oil, water, and egg, and mix until smooth and creamy. Add the mixture to the flour on low just until the dough forms. Divide into 4 equal-sized balls, and chill for 15 to 20 minutes.

Pie: Roll out one of the balls of pastry into an 11-inch circle on a well-floured surface. Carefully lift the rolled pastry dough, using a large pastry knife, remove off the surface, and fold in half. Place it across one side of the pie dish, and unfold across the other side of the pie dish. Repeat for the top of pie, but roll out into an 11½" circle. In a bowl, combine about 5 to 6 cups of peeled, diced or sliced apples and pears, sugar, lemon, cinnamon, nutmeg, salt, flour and tapioca. Mix the apple mixture well, and fill the pastry-lined pie pan with the apples. Dot with butter. Cover the pie by placing the top pastry crust on the pie like the bottom one, seal, and flute edge. Paint the top of the pie with water, and sprinkle with sugar. Cut 4 slits for the steam to escape. Bake for 20 minutes; reduce oven to 375, and continue cooking for about 25 minutes. Check the pie for browning about every 5 to 10 minutes after that. When the pie becomes golden brown, cover the pie with foil to keep the pie from becoming too brown, and continue cooking. Let cool before cutting. Yield: 8 to 10 cuts | Recipe by Chef Bo

Cannoli Filling

2 cups ricotta cheese; preferably whole milk
3/4 cup powdered sugar
1 teaspoon vanilla
1/4 cup heavy cream

Optional to stir in or garnish with:
1/4 cup small semisweet chocolate chips
1/4 cup pistachios; chopped
16 sugar wafer cones

In a medium bowl, whisk the ricotta until smooth. Sift in the powdered sugar; add vanilla, ther to blend. In a separate bowl, or in the bowl of an electric mixer fitted with the whisk attachn beat the heavy cream until fairly stiff. Using a rubber spatula, gently fold the whipped cream the ricotta mixture. Refrigerate for 2 to 3 hours before using. Can store up to three days in refrigerator. A great cannoli starts with a great shell.

Yield: 8 cannolis or 16 cones | Recipe by Chef Bo

Carrot Cake

3 cups all-purpose flour
3 cups white sugar
3 teaspoons ground cinnamon
1/2 teaspoon baking soda
1½ teaspoons baking powder
1/2 teaspoon salt
1½ cups vegetable oil
5 eggs; beaten
2 teaspoons vanilla extract

3 cups carrots; grated
1½ cups crushed pineapple; slightly drained
1¼ cups golden raisins
1 cup pecans or walnuts; chopped
Cream Cheese Frosting:
2 tablespoons soft butter
8 ounces cream cheese
1 teaspoon vanilla
3 cups confectioners' sugar

Preheat oven to 350 degrees. Mix all the dry ingredients, blend in oil, eggs, and vanilla, and stir well. Add carrots, pineapple, raisins, and pecans, and stir well. Grease and flour two 10-inch round cake pans. Pour evenly into the prepared pans. Bake for 38 to 40 minutes in the preheated oven until cake tests done with a toothpick. Cool for 15 or more minutes before removing from pan. The frosting: In a medium mixing bowl, combine butter, cream cheese, vanilla, and confectioners' sugar. Blend until creamy. When cake is completely cooled, frost with the frosting.

Yield: 12 cuts | Recipe by Chef Bo

Cinnamon Streusel Zucchini Bread

1 cup fresh zucchini; finely shredded
2 eggs
1/2 cup vegetable oil
1/2 cup plain Greek yogurt
1 teaspoon vanilla extract
1½ cups all-purpose flour
3/4 cup granulated sugar
1 teaspoon baking powder
1/2 teaspoon salt
1/2 teaspoon cinnamon
1/4 teaspoon nutmeg

For cinnamon swirl:
1/4 teaspoon granulated sugar
1/4 teaspoon cinnamon
For the streusel topping:
3 tablespoons flour
1/4 cup brown sugar
1/4 teaspoon cinnamon
2 tablespoons unsalted butter;
    slightly softened and cut into pieces
1/2 cup nuts; chopped;
    (walnuts and pecans work well)

Preheat oven to 350 degrees. Spray a 9x5 loaf pan with cooking spray, and set aside. In a large mixing bowl, combine zucchini, eggs, oil, yogurt, and vanilla. Mix thoroughly to combine. In a separate bowl, combine flour, sugar, baking powder, salt, cinnamon, and nutmeg. Gradually sift the dry ingredients into the wet, and stir the batter just until all the ingredients are fully incorporated. Don't overmix. In a small bowl, combine the cinnamon and sugar to create the cinnamon swirl. Pour the batter into the prepared pan. Top with the cinnamon sugar. Using a knife, run it up and down the pan and side to side through the batter to create a swirl. Add the flour, brown sugar, and cinnamon in a medium bowl, and mix until combined. Cut in the butter using a fork or a pastry blender until it resembles coarse crumbs. Stir in chopped nuts (I use 1/4 cup pecans and 1/4 cup walnuts). Sprinkle the streusel topping evenly over the batter. Bake the bread for 1 hour to 1 hour 10 minutes, or until a toothpick inserted into the center of the loaf comes out clean. Remove from oven, and cool 10 to 5 minutes in the pan on a wire rack. Remove the bread from the pan, and continue to cool on the wire rack. Serve warm or at room temperature.

Yield: one loaf pan | Recipe by Chef Bo

Date Nut Pinwheel Cookies

1 cup butter; softened
1 cup sugar
1 cup brown sugar; packed
2 large eggs; room temperature
4 cups all-purpose flour
1/2 teaspoon baking soda

Filling:
2 (8-ounce) packages pitted dates
1 cup water
1/2 cup sugar
1/2 cup walnuts; chopped

You can add food coloring to the dough at Christmastime.

In a large bowl, cream butter and sugars. Beat in eggs. In another bowl, whisk flour and baking soda, and gradually beat into creamed mixture. Divide dough into 3 portions, and shape each into a ball. Cover and refrigerate 1 hour or until firm enough to roll. For filling: Place dates, water, and sugar in a large saucepan, and bring to a boil. Reduce heat, and simmer uncovered until dates are tender and liquid is almost evaporated. Stir in walnuts, and cool completely. Roll each dough portion between 2 sheets of waxed paper into a 12x10-inch rectangle. Refrigerate for 30 minutes. Remove waxed paper, and spread a third of the filling over each rectangle. Roll up tightly jellyroll-style, starting with a long side. Wrap securely, and refrigerate until firm. Preheat oven to 350 degrees. Unwrap, and cut dough crosswise into 1/3-inch slices. Place 2 inches apart on greased baking sheets. Bake 10-12 minutes or until set. Remove from pans, and place on wire racks to cool.

Yield: 20 to 30 Cookies | Recipe by Chef Bo

Rainbow Cookies

4 egg yolks
8 ounces butter; room temperature
1 cup sugar
3/4-pound almond paste; broken up into
   small chunks
2 cups all-purpose flour

4 egg whites
Food coloring: green and red
Large jar of apricot jam
4 to 6 ounces semisweet baker's chocolate

In a stand mixer, add egg yolks and butter, and mix well. Add sugar, and mix well. Add the almond paste, and mix well (Break up the almond paste in small chunks before adding it to the mixer so that it mixes quicker). Add the flour, and mix well. Beat the egg whites with a fork until they get a little foamy, and add them to the mixer. Mix for a few minutes until you have a soft and uniform dough. Divide the dough into 3 equal parts, and place in three separate bowls. The dough in one bowl should be left white. The dough in another bowl should be colored green, and the other one red. Add as much food coloring as you like until you get the color tone that you prefer. Evenly spread the mixes in three separate ungreased 8x12-inch aluminum baking sheets. Bake each one at 375 degrees for 10-12 minutes. Let them all cool off. Put a piece of parchment paper on a wood board, and deposit the green sheet. Spread a thin layer of apricot jam over the entire surface of the green sheet. Place the white sheet on top of the green sheet. Spread apricot jam on the white surface as well. Deposit the red sheet over the white and, with your hands, press well so that the three sheets will stick together. With a serrated knife, trim all four edges of the tricolor sheets. Melt the chocolate, and spread it over the top of the sheets. Let the chocolate dry, preferably overnight. Turn upside down, and spread melted chocolate over the other side. Let the chocolate dry, and cut the cookies into pieces of about 1½ x ½ inches or as big as you prefer.

Yield: 2-1/2 dozen | Recipe by Chef Bo

Ricotta Lemon Drop Cookies

2½ cups all-purpose flour
1 teaspoon baking powder
3/4 teaspoon sea salt
2 eggs
2 cups sugar
1 teaspoon vanilla extract or the seeds from 1 vanilla bean
1/2 cup extra-virgin olive oil
1 pound whole milk ricotta cheese

Juice from 1 lemon
Zest from 1 lemon

For the lemon glaze:
1 large lemon; juice and zest
2 cups confectioners' sugar or
    more as needed
1/4 cup poppy seeds; optional

Preheat your oven to 375 degrees. In a large mixing bowl, whisk together the flour, baking powder, and sea salt. Set aside. In a separate bowl, whisk together the egg with the sugar, vanilla extract, and olive oil until creamy. Add the ricotta cheese, and whisk until incorporated. Whisk in the juice and zest, then pour all the wet ingredients on top of the flour mixture. Using a spatula, fold the wet mixture into the dry until combined. Line two baking sheets with parchment paper and, using two spoons, drop the cookie dough by spoonful on the sheet, leaving about a 1½ inch space in between. Bake the ricotta cookies in the preheated oven for about 17 to 20 minutes until golden brown around the edges. Using a small cookie spatula, transfer them to a cooling rack. Once the ricotta cookies have cooled off completely, make your lemon glaze by whisking together the juice from 1 lemon with the powdered sugar. Add more confectioners' sugar if needed until desired consistency is achieved. Using a small spoon, add some of the glaze to each ricotta cookie, and sprinkle with the reserved lemon zest and poppy seeds. Allow the glaze to set for about 45 minutes.

Yield: 25 cookies | Recipe by Chef Bo

A super-easy ricotta cookie recipe, made with olive oil (no butter) and whole milk ricotta cheese. Crispy on the bottom and fluffy in the center with a decadent lemon glaze and poppy seed sprinkle. Store in an airtight container.

Ricotta Cheese Cookies

1 cup (2 sticks) butter; softened
2 cups sugar
1 pound ricotta cheese
2 teaspoons vanilla extract
2 large eggs
4 cups all-purpose flour
2 tablespoons baking powder
1/2 teaspoon salt

Glaze (icing):
1½ cups confectioners' sugar
3 tablespoons milk
Red or green sugar crystals; optional

Preheat oven to 350 degrees. In large bowl on low, beat sugar and butter until blended. Increase speed to high, and cream about 5 minutes. Add ricotta, vanilla, and eggs until well combined at a medium speed. On low, add flour, baking powder, and salt. Beat until dough forms. Drop dough by level tablespoons, about 2 inches apart, onto ungreased large cookie sheet. Bake about 15 minutes or until cookies are very lightly golden (cookies will be soft and cakelike). When the cookies are cool, prepare icing by mixing confectioners' sugar and milk until smooth. Spread icing on cookies, and sprinkle with red or green sugar crystals. Let dry for 1 to 4 hours.

Yield: 6 dozen | Recipe by Chef Bo

Wedding Cookies

1 cup butter; softened
1 cup confectioners' sugar
1 teaspoon vanilla extract
2 cups cake flour
1 cup pecans; chopped
1/2 cup or more confectioners' sugar for rolling

Preheat the oven to 325 degrees. In a large bowl, cream together butter, confectioners' sugar, and vanilla until smooth. Stir in the cake flour, then fold in the pecans. Roll dough into 1-inch balls, and place them 1 inch apart onto ungreased cookie sheets. Bake for 15 to 18 minutes in the preheated oven, until lightly browned. Cool cookies completely, and roll in additional confectioners' sugar.

If you are storing the cookies in a tin, add any remaining sugar to the tin. Store airtight at room temperature. The cookies freeze well. Don't try to double unless you've got a really big mixer!

Yield: about 40 cookies | Recipe by Chef Bo

White Chocolate and Almond Biscotti

2¾ cups all-purpose flour
1½ cups sugar
1½ teaspoons baking powder
1 teaspoon salt
1/2 cup almonds; chopped

1/2 cup white baking chocolate; chopped
2 eggs
2 egg yolks
6 tablespoons butter; melted

Preheat oven to 325 degrees. Grease two large cookie sheets, or line with parchment paper. In your mixing bowl, combine flour, sugar, baking powder, and salt. Blend the flour mixture. On low, stir in almonds and baking chocolate, add eggs and egg yolks, and mix. Add butter and mix until combined into dough; the dough will be crumbly. Use your hands to knead dough until it comes together. Divide dough into 3 equal parts. Place 1/3 of dough on cookie sheet, and form into logs about 14 inches long and about 1-1/2 to 2 inches wide. Place each log about 3 inches apart. Bake 25 to 30 minutes in the preheated oven until very lightly brown. Cool for 15 minutes, transfer logs to a cutting board, and cut diagonally into 1/2-inch slices. Arrange slices on cookie sheet cut-side down, and continue baking 10 minutes. Turn them over, and bake 10 to 12 minutes more or until crisp, then let cool. Cool cookies on wire racks. Store airtight at room temperature; the cookies freeze well.

Yield: 60 Biscotti | Recipe by Chef Bo

Appendix

Appendix

Let's Cook Something Good

Appendix